LOOKING FOR THE FUTURE

*A personal connection to
yesterday's great expectations,
today's reality, and tomorrow's hope*

Karen,
a favorite of
mine. a friend
with a conscience!
Leo

LEON WOFSY

Cover photos by Jane Scherr
Front: An anti-Apartheid demonstration in 1986 on the
Berkeley Campus of the University of California
Back: Leon Wofsy, 1994

ISBN 0-9644667-0-8
Library of Congress Catalogue Number: 94-69978

I W ROSE PRESS

Available from:

Institute for Social and Economic Studies
P.O.Box 2809, Oakland CA 94609
(510) 843-7495

LOOKING FOR THE FUTURE

Leon Wofsy

TO ROZ

ACKNOWLEDGEMENTS

My thanks go to friends and family members who read drafts of the manuscript and gave me encouragement and critical comments. Included are Roz, Carla, David and the grandchildren; also Max Elbaum, Lester Rodney, Barbara Christian, Ed Hoffman, Alan Wald, David Englestein, Jeanette and Nat Brooks, Bob Blauner, Robby Cohen, colleagues from the Faculty Committee for Human Rights in Central America, and some dear, fellow old alums from the Labor Youth League. Thanks also to Fred Taub, who offered his time and expertise (and patience with me) to the design and production of this book.

NEW YORK, THURSDAY, MAY 8, 1930

SUBSCRIPTION RATES and Bronx, New York

Assaulted at Stamford May Day Demonstration, Then Beaten in Jail

Seated, left to right: Henry Scott, Anthony Lalama, Joseph Nevin, Charles McMahn, Morris Fitch, Morris Rankin.

Standing, left to right: Isaac Lifkin, I. Wofsy, A. Nachowitz, Phil Kaufman, Louis Tomilio. All are held for trial under a total bail of $10,000.

These workers were made to run the gauntlet between two lines of 50 police each at the jail. They were then taken to cells, and led out one at a time to be beaten with brass kunckles, iron manacles, and lead pipes. Morris Fitch, Negro worker, was beaten three times in succession, being flung headlong into a cell between times. Then the police tried to blind him by poking their fingers in his eyes. When this did not bring either a whine or whimper from him, they took off his shoes and beat him on the ankles with iron weapons. He refused to flinch.

The uniformed thugs doing most of the torturing are: Carl Paight, Lester Hay and others known. Police Chief Jack Brennen and Captain George McCarthy personally supervi' it.

Photo from the *Daily Worker*. Isadore Wofsy, Leon's father, is standing second from the left.

FOREWORD

Now, as when I was a child some sixty years ago, I think of my father as very special. I remember a person who was honest, modest, and wise. It wasn't his fault that the promise he made to his children proved beyond reach. We grew up convinced that our generation would see America turn to socialism. Someday we would live in a gentle world where wars and exploitation had become unthinkable. My mother, too, shared the hope, although she was the skeptic—always a rebel, never the true believer. Our parents gave themselves and all their days to the future, and we shared their commitment proudly.

Not only the promise, but our image of a better world in birth was treated rudely by 20th Century reality. The noblest, but also some of the basest, endowments of human experience found expression in the movement that pioneered socialist revolution in our time.

For as long as I may be around, it will still be too soon to say, as Lincoln Steffens did after visiting the Soviet Union in the 1920s: "I have seen the future and it works!" Yet I wonder. Does the experience of my generation's years lead somewhere? Is current reality, however removed from early dreams, the serious beginning of transition to a better world? That is what I want to explore in this book. I want to look at how the world and my perceptions of it have changed, and to gain some feeling for where history is heading. This may be "mission impossible," but the excuse for my journey is not a sense of mission. It is an impulse, born of a lifetime addiction to the future.

The reliving I'll do in these pages will not be stretched to accommodate my addiction. Some reminiscences are just for their own sake, sharing stories with the grandchildren rather than musing about posterity. Still, the memories that make up the first part of this book are meant as a prelude to the reflections that follow. The self-sketch is therefore more a summary of relevant personal political history than an all-around memoir.

June 9, 1994:

The Foreword was written and the manuscript begun in late 1991. The text has not been updated to reflect events that happened after a particular section was completed. I want to leave a feeling for the process, my personal difficulty in trying to integrate old and new experience in a strange, unsettled post-Cold War world.

PART I

WHERE I'VE TRAVELED

CHAPTER 1

BORN RED

I was eye witness to an electric moment in 1951. Relived since on countless radio and TV replays, Bobby Thomson's home run won the pennant for the New York Giants at the last possible moment, after all had seemed lost. What I remember most is the instant in which the crowd was transformed, the faces of Dodger fans turning in a flash from the joy of certain victory to deepest despair, while Giant faces panned in the same split second from defeat to ecstasy.

For me, the Giants' home field Polo Grounds was the perfect place to be on that day. It broke the tension of what we used to call being "unavailable" during the McCarthy period. I remained securely sheltered from the FBI, anonymous in a vast crowd, while the Giants ("my team" since I first saw Carl Hubbell pitch in 1933) made baseball history.

At that time, I was the Communist Party's designated youth leader. From 1949 to 1956, I was National Chairman of the Labor Youth League. No one who had known me in my childhood and teen years during the nineteen thirties would have found that surprising.

On March 6th, 1930 and again on May 1st, 1930, my father, Isadore Wofsy, was arrested for "demonstrating without a permit." The cause was unemployment insurance and social security, not yet recognized in the law of the land. Permits were applied for and denied, but thousands demonstrated anyway in our small town of Stamford, Connecticut. I was 8 years old and very proud of my father. He was the principal leader of the huge movement that sprang up in Stamford at the onset of the Great Depression, as it did all over the USA.

In Stamford, as almost everywhere else, local police followed the lead of the Hoover Administration in meeting demonstrations with violence. My father's first cousin, Abraham, was a judge in Stamford. He and my father, both immigrants who left Czarist Russia before the First World War, had been close friends. After the March 6th arrest, the Judge sent a message to my father warning that if there was another demonstration, the police would be out to punish him. The May 1st demonstration filled every corner of the town square and went through without incident, except for the arrest of my father and twelve others who tried to speak from different vantage points in the crowd. But once inside the police station, the arrestees were taken from their cells one at a time and savagely beaten with blackjacks and brass knuckles by a team of four police. Morris Fitch, an African-American, refused to scream and the violence mounted until a jaw and an ankle were broken. Sixty-five year-old Charlie McMahn Smith suffered a broken arm. My father had a deep gash over an eye, and received a body stomping that crippled him for weeks. Rose Bloom was mistaken for my mother, but out of deference for women, she was only slapped repeatedly about the face and cursed with obscenities. All were left for hours without medical attention. When word of what had happened leaked out, my mother got our family doctor to demand entry to the jail.

This episode was made even more indelible on my childhood memory because my brother, Malcolm, and I were suspended from school (he was in the eighth grade, I in the fourth) for staying out on May 1st. That year President Herbert Hoover proclaimed May 1st Child Health Day, and school administrators decided that pupils absent in observance of the Workers' Holiday would be suspended. Our suspension was terminated after several days when we and our parents (my father heavily bandaged) made the obligatory appearance before the Stamford Superintendent of Schools. My mother spoke for us, and far from contrition, her message was "J'accuse!" Hers was one of the first Jewish families to settle in Stamford, at the beginning of the century. She reminded the superintendent that she knew him and Police Chief Brennan as children, when they were running after her father's horse and buggy, throwing stones and shouting "kike."

The case against the "illegal" demonstrators was thrown out, but not until it got to the Appeals Court. During the initial trial, our cousin, the Judge, absented himself from Stamford. He and my father never saw each other again.

I was the youngest of three children. My sister, Clare, sixteen years older, was the child of a prior marriage that began when our mother, Rose Gordon, was eighteen and ended after two years. My parents married during the First World War. Malcolm was born in 1917, and I, in 1921. Clare was married and out of the house by the time I was seven. She never met her father after infancy, and her bond with my father became close, stronger through the years.

Our mother was only three years old when she came to this country from Russia. She was the youngest of nine children, one of two girls in an orthodox family that believed education was for males only. She left home in rebellion, but never got the chance to go to school after the eighth grade. Instead, she educated herself, became a lifelong avid reader and a remarkably knowledgeable lover of the classics in literature and music.

Rose and Izzy were both loving and completely devoted parents, yet each had quite different things to give. In many ways theirs was a marriage of opposites, something no one could miss.

Rose made everyone around her a lover of music, novels and poetry. She comes to life for me when I recall my first passionate discovery of Beethoven's *Fifth* or Mozart's *Exultate Jubilate,* Romain Roland's *Jean Christophe* or O'Henry's *Gift of the Magi.* She was a romantic, unhappy that life never gave her the chance to train her beautiful voice and explore her potential in music. She was also outspoken, undisciplined in her frankness, quick to find fault. When someone took offense, she would feel miserable. Afterward she would say "I am my own worst enemy," but she could never contain her reactions for the sake of tact.

Izzy was the revolutionary activist, but everyone said he could never hurt a fly. He credited a socialist barber for his recruitment to socialism soon after he came to America as a sixteen year-old. He was an active supporter of Eugene V. Debs in his opposition to World War I, and he became a founding member of the Communist Party after the war. His life was committed to the cause before he met Rose, and nothing ever would change that. He, too, was an avid reader, but his reading was newspapers, political articles, Marxist pamphlets and books. He participated with Rose in Jewish folk choruses, and he loved family sing-alongs as we rode together in the car, but cultural pursuits were not his passion. He was inhibited and conservative in his personal carriage and behavior. He was fluent in Yiddish, but he curbed his use of it so that he could learn to think routinely in English and become a more effective organizer and public speaker. In contrast to his political determination, he was very gentle and tolerant of people. Persuasion rather than arm twisting was his way with the children and, remarkably, in Party activities (even in frenetic fund drives).

How did they get along? Not smoothly, not without below-the-surface resentments and conflict. Each was deeply admiring of the other. Each, though, could blame the other for difficulties and embarrassments, and neither ever could really adjust to the other's faults. Of course the bargain was worse for Rose, for even liberated women were expected to put the man's work first. And Rose did, willingly, despite her independent ways.

My earliest memories in Stamford, Connecticut include two occasions when I learned about death, about victims and martyrs of social injustice. I held my father's hand as the family waited in silence and sorrow on the Town Hall steps for the word that finally came of the execution of Sacco and Vanzetti, the immigrant Italian anarchists framed on a murder charge and posthumously exonerated decades later by the State of Massachusetts. Then there was the day we joined others at the railroad station as the train that carried the body of Harry Simms stopped on its way to Springfield, Massachusetts. Harry was a Young Communist Leaguer from "our District," a teenager who volunteered as an organizer of mine workers in bloody Harlan County, Kentucky, and was shot to death by hired company thugs. We knew him as Harry Hersch.

In 1932, the family moved from Stamford, Connecticut to New Haven, where my father was to serve as District Organizer for the Communist Party in Connecticut and western Massachusetts. For me, as a child, the depression was real and personal. I was skinny and had asthma. I still feel the cold of those winters when we couldn't heat the house, when my parents couldn't pay the rent, when there was too little milk and no oranges, when a stew of lung and other organ meats at two cents a pound was our frequent main meal. We had comrades, though, no better or worse off than we—doors were never locked and sharing was simply comradeship.

These were good years for the movement. Our family felt itself part of new times in the making. Often, especially when I was in high school, I rode with my father as he drove up and down the District in a Model A Ford, the Party's car which we called "the Old Gray Mare." He met and planned with organizers who were building new industrial unions that would form the CIO. We walked spirited picket lines, singing union and revolutionary songs, preaching and practicing unity between workers black and white. I listened to him in public debates with local politicians when he ran for Governor on the Communist ticket in 1936.

The movement also spread among intellectuals. We formed close friendships with professors and students at Yale and at Smith College. What we called "mass work" thrived in Connecticut. Independent political action became strong through Labor's Non-Partisan League and the Connecticut Conference on Labor and Legislative Action. Connecticut gave its share of Lincoln Battalion volunteers to the anti-fascist cause in Loyalist Spain. A dear family friend, Dewitt Parker, was one of many who didn't come back.

Active participation on my own began in Hillhouse High School, 1934-1938. Of course, before that, I was a Young Pioneer—I even spoke at a rally with James Ford, Communist candidate for Vice President in 1932, declaiming to Hoover and Roosevelt that "workers' children want bread, not beer!"

(Then, in my seat on the platform, I lost a desperate battle to stay awake.) But in high school, my own initiative led to a sizable Peace Council and affiliation with the radical American Student Union. Outside school, my friends and I picketed a local swimming pool where we were denied entry because some were black. My co-leader in that action was a black woman student at Hillhouse High who in later years became an outstanding civil rights attorney and a federal judge.

When I graduated from high school, the college I chose (the only one I would consider) was New York's City College (CCNY). True, tuition was free, and academically it was superior. The chief attraction for me was its reputation as the premier campus for radical student activity. My brother was there, working nights to support himself, and with him I set up the required New York residence.

In the years preceding my arrival at CCNY, large protest demonstrations—particularly one against the City's welcome for a large Italian fascist air armada—resulted in the expulsion of many students, some of whom soon became leading Communist organizers and journalists. Some went from CCNY to fight fascism in Spain.

At CCNY, I became President of the Marxist Cultural Society and then leader of the Young Communist League. My college years, 1938-1942, were overwhelmed by the inexorable process that exploded into World War II. These were times of intellectual and emotional torment as students followed the zigzags of pre-war diplomacy, especially the rapid swings in Communist policies.

My comrades and I gathered at lunch time in Alcove 2 of the campus cafeteria, where we held daily current events sessions. There were no formal speeches, just questions and answers, and dialogue open to anyone who cared to debate— anyone, that is, except the Trotskyists whose hang-out was next door in Alcove 1. In my eyes, Trotskyists were almost as evil as fascists, and fraternizing would have been a sin. Looking back, we young Communists brought together a strange mixture of lively, logical minds and dogmatic beliefs. We were tireless activists and effective social critics, ready to question anything except our faith in Soviet socialism. Alcove 1 included at one time or another Irving Howe, Irving Kristol, Seymour Martin Lipset, and numerous other budding intellectuals, many of whom were eventually to turn against their youthful radicalism. Their dogmatism at CCNY was the inverse of ours, their positions on the war, anti-fascist unity and everything else being dominated first of all by opposition to anything the Communists supported.

A few years ago, Irving Kristol, now an ardent conservative, wrote nostalgically about Alcove 1 in an article for the *New York Times Magazine.* He boasted about the successful careers that emerged from his milieu at CCNY, in contrast to only two notable individuals from Alcove 2: Julius Rosenberg and a scientist on the faculty of a Western university (presumably me). I could lengthen the latter list by several names, but Kristol's imbalance in "success" was produced by what happened *after* graduation, especially during Cold War McCarthyism. His reference to Julius Rosenberg, executed with his wife, Ethel, in the most shameful home-front atrocity of the Korean War, is ironic and relevant. The story of careers aborted, sidetracked, or delayed when McCarthyism swept academia is recounted in detail in Ellen Schrecker's book, *No Ivory Tower.* The problem was hardly any intellectual lack in "our" undergraduates, for some of the brightest and most cultured young scholars simply found themselves excluded from university faculties in the 1950s.

(One such case was that of my brother, Malcolm. After his four years of military service in World War II, he achieved his

Ph.D. degree and earned an academic position as Assistant Professor of Biochemistry at the University of Wisconsin. His appointment was terminated unexpectedly soon after he became one of the principal leaders of the "Joe Must Go" movement against Wisconsin Senator Joseph McCarthy. By chance, in 1984, Malcolm and I met the son of his former department chairman. The young man told us about a case of academic blacklisting which his guilt-ridden father had confided to him many years ago. He didn't know when he began the story that its subject was Malcolm.)

After the Hitler-Stalin Non-Aggression Pact, one of the periodic waves of anti-Red hysteria targeted the faculty at New York's City Colleges. In 1940, the Rapp-Coudert investigation, New York State's antecedent of the McCarthy witch-hunts, got twelve CCNY professors fired. I was a Junior, and that was certainly a busy year for me, so busy that I had little time for classes and dropped most of my courses. We organized three very large protest rallies coupled with one-day student strikes, bigger and more spirited than any student actions I know of until the Free Speech Movement at Berkeley in 1964.

My choice of academic major in my first two years was English literature, but I switched to chemistry as the practical choice for getting a job after graduation. My sole career ambition was to work for the movement. When I graduated, however, there was only one objective, to serve in the anti-fascist war. I was drafted in the Army after persuading the medical examiner, who initially rejected me because of chronic bronchial asthma, that I felt healthy enough for full service. Less than a year later, an asthma attack, while I was stationed in Augusta, Georgia, put me in the hospital and resulted in a medical discharge.

My short army hitch was not entirely uneventful. My nose was broken by an MP in my barracks during basic training in

Texas because I objected to his boasts of manhandling the "niggers" while he was on duty in Harlem. When I was stationed in Georgia, I was sent to Specialist Training School at the Citadel in South Carolina, but before training began, I was abruptly removed and brought back under guard to my base camp in Augusta. During my ten days or so at the Citadel, my mail was crudely steamed open before it came to my hands. About thirty five years later, my FBI files established that I was the subject of an Army Intelligence investigation. The investigators reported that all "witnesses" of my Army performance testified favorably about my character and patriotism, but one derogatory item was cited. It was a quote from a letter sent to me and pre-screened at the Citadel. A friend wrote that, while she was a tuberculosis patient at a sanitarium in New Jersey, she had seen French troops march by and observed no color bar; and wasn't it "a shame that in our democracy the army is segregated."

For a few months before my Army time, and again for a few months after, I worked as a technician in organic chemistry and pharmaceutical laboratories. But in May, 1944, I became an organizer for the American Youth for Democracy in the Bronx. That began a stretch of twelve years as a full-time organizer for a succession of youth organizations associated with the Communist movement.

Rosalind Taub and I had married on my twenty-first birthday in November, 1942. As I write this, Roz and I are in our fiftieth anniversary year. We picked each other out from a large circle of Hunter girls and City College boys who were often together at parties, meetings, and "musicals." (The "musicals" were gatherings in homes to listen, often for the first time, to a recording of a great symphony or concerto.) We shared the same dreams about what young Communists called "life with a purpose." We knew things would be tough, but we wanted to be a family. Our two children were soon born, Carla in May, 1944 and David in December, 1946. Carla was conceived in a mattress storage room of an army hospital, when Roz came to wait with me while my medical discharge papers were being completed.

We have always had reason to be happy with the kids, happy that they came along while we were youthful, energetic, and very excited about our lives. We were scared when we first brought Carla home. I remember adding to my complaints about society: how could "they" abruptly leave the care of a precious, helpless infant to such unprepared and incompetent parents? Once the panic subsided, we were very willing and involved parents. Carla and, later, David were always at the center of our world no matter its twists and turns. We wanted them not only to feel our love, but to share what was happening in our lives and beyond. We learned that even a young child can notice and want to understand something of social values and conditions in the outer world. Carla, at age three, scanned the crowd as we waited on line at a public swimming pool, and asked in a whisper if it was all right to speak of people as "chocolate" or "vanilla." When I had to leave home to be "unavailable" or on organizing trips, David would comfort his tearful older sister while Roz and I explained the "good things" our family was trying to do. I don't think the children ever felt left out or sacrificed to a bigger cause. In any case, as the children grew to adolescence and into their own adult lives, we never had to experience the retaliation of resentment and alienation that was the ultimate price in pain for some radical activist parents.

The Labor Youth League (LYL) was formed in May, 1949 when the Cold War was in full cry. Its history was dominated by the rise of McCarthyism and the effort to fight back. This was the time of Smith Act trials and imprisonment of Communists, Korean War hysteria, the Attorney General's List, the trial and execution of Julius and Ethel Rosenberg, the bloody assault on Paul Robeson's Peekskill Concert, countless punitive sorties by the McCarthy and UnAmerican Committees, the McCarran Act inquisitions, and lots more. Millions were stigmatized and badgered, driven from jobs and professions, even shunned by friends who feared "guilt by association." The vast majority who were caught in the buckshot of McCarthyism had no connection with Communists, perhaps a "past" or peripheral link with left or liberal activity. Conformity became the measure of "loyalty" throughout the country. This was particularly unhealthy for young people. Youth is by nature curious and rebellious, but youth of the '50s were dubbed "the Silent Generation."

Nevertheless, in LYL, our spirits were high, and we were quite undaunted in our campaigns against McCarthyism, racism, and nuclear war. The high mark in LYL membership was about 5,000. Two things stand out in my LYL memories. One is being a target of the witch hunters. The other is the quality of my young friends and comrades.

I remember many occasions when a pair of FBI agents would suddenly confront me on the street. Most impressive was the time I kissed my seven year-old daughter as I left her at school, and suddenly experienced the FBI men hovering over me. "You love your family, don't you? Do you want to stay with them?" As they followed me down the street, one agent cajoled that he was only trying to help me, while the other cursed my silence with a crescendo of vicious threats.

We in LYL benefited from the Justice Department's choice of tactics in dealing with us as leaders of a youth organization. We were processed under the McCarran Act, rather than being arrested and jailed under the Smith Act. Many years later, both acts were ruled unconstitutional by the Supreme Court, but the irreversible toll on individuals was much more extreme for Smith Act victims. The Smith Act sought essentially to outlaw the Communist Party, and hundreds of Party functionaries and local leaders were arrested, many jailed, some driven underground and later imprisoned for five years or more. The McCarran Act subjected organizations listed as "subversive" by the Attorney General to prosecutory hearings aimed at compelling the officers to turn over membership lists, or be jailed for "contempt." Actually the penalties prescribed under McCarran were even more outlandish than under Smith, five years in jail and a $5,000 fine for each day (!) of refusal to register membership. But the process involved prolonged hearings before a registration order became final, and it turned out that there was sufficient time for the political climate to change and the inquisition to be aborted.

That outcome was not predictable during the early '50s. Our family of four moved together with Roz's brother, Leon Taub, and his wife, Rena. The idea was to provide for the probability that I would be among those arrested or forced to leave home. With Rena giving care to our children after school hours, and later to her own new baby, Roz was able to take a job as a nursery school teacher.

The House UnAmerican Activities Committee soon began issuing subpoenas to heads of "front" organizations, also aimed at forcing membership list disclosures. That prompted a decision that I should leave home and go "unavailable" for a period of about four months in 1951. Eventually we concluded that it was a mistake for the Chair of LYL to be in hiding.

Soon I had my turn in Washington before the UnAmerican Committee. With Congressman Francis Walter presiding, I refused to answer questions under the First and Fifth Amendments. That was the standard ritual for avoiding a Hobson's choice, naming names or being prosecuted on a "contempt" charge for refusing to be an informer. During an intermission, a large group of church youth spectators were being told by their tour guide that I would not have refused answers to the Committee if I had nothing to hide. I joined the group and volunteered that I would answer any questions about my beliefs and affiliations to them directly, but not to the Committee's inquisitors. When Walter returned to the hearing room and saw what was going on, he raged, "Throw the bum out!" The security guard who ushered me out of the building was embarrassed and whispered an apology.

My major face-off with the inquisition came in 1953-54 when Attorney General Herbert Brownell ordered the LYL before the Subversive Activities Control Board (SACB) under the McCarran Act. As National Chairman, I was the primary witness at the hearing. That meant three days of direct testimony and eight days of cross examination by the government prosecutor, Kirk Maddrix. Maddrix had been prosecutor in the unsuccessful case of the *U.S. v. W.E.B. Du Bois,* the great African-American statesman and philosopher. The sole presiding officer appointed by the SACB, the man who alone could decide whether LYL was "subversive" under the terms of the McCarran Act, was ex-Senator Harry P. Cain. The AFL-CIO had named Senator Cain as labor's "public enemy number one," describing him as "viciously anti-labor and also one of the Senate's loudest apologists for Joe McCarthy."

SACB hearings were run differently than Smith Act trials, where defendants were harshly prevented from discussing their views and jailed for "contempt" if they persisted. SACB witnesses were badgered repeatedly, but were given more lee-way than those subpoenaed by the House UnAmerican or McCarthy Senate committees. The object of the hearing was not on-the-spot punishment of individuals, but to lay the "legal" basis for *de facto* outlawing of an organization. It was important to the government to make the SACB proceedings appear fair, probably because the McCarran Act was poten-tially so vulnerable on constitutional grounds.

When I look back over the testimony, my own and that of the three other LYL witnesses, I'm glad we spoke and acted as we did during the McCarthy period. We stood up without apologies to a crowd that was intimidating the country, and that would be recognized belatedly as lacking all decency. We did, of course, believe and say a few things that I now see as naive or dogmatic, actually foolish. Still our words and actions were an articulate, deeply felt commitment to democracy, racial equality, and social justice.

A strange sequel to the McCarran drama was revealed more than two decades later when I got my FBI files. Included was a "prosecutory file," showing that my father and I had been among twenty-two people (all the other names were blacked out) targeted nationally for arrest when the McCarran Act verdicts were validated by the courts. Then there was a bizarre exchange of internal FBI letters in 1961, before the Supreme Court threw out the Act. By then I was a biologist at the University of California in San Diego (this narrative will soon tell what brought me there). I was forty years old and more than five years out of the Labor Youth League. The San Diego Bureau of the FBI wrote to Washington that the passage of time and my changed circumstances made it advisable to drop me from the list of twenty-two scheduled for indictment. The return letter, signed by J. Edgar Hoover himself, agreed to drop my name, but asked the San Diego office to suggest another to replace mine!

Lifelong friendships were born in the LYL, although we were soon to go different ways. Impossible as it seemed to us then, the bond that some of us had with the Communist Party would break or fade away. Yet the adversity that McCarthyism fashioned bred comradeship and affection among us, and a conscience that would always keep most of us involved in movements and ideas of social change. We were far from alone, or even as important as others, in resisting the scourge. Still we shared our youth, our poverty, periods of separation and abnormal living for our families and children. (For some the disruption was far longer and more severe than anything Roz and I and our children had to face.)

Nostalgia brings two other attributes of our comradeship to mind. First, a large number of our leaders and members were African-American, and the close interaction of black and white anticipated some of the spirit of the approaching civil rights upsurge. Second, the small and besieged Labor Youth League attracted a surprising number of young talents. The first one to remember is Lorraine Hansberry, who wrote *Raisin in the Sun* and, in a short life, put so much beauty and insight into words. Our Harlem organizer, and a fellow witness in the SACB hearings, was Douglas Turner Ward, future playwright, actor, director and founder of the Negro Ensemble Theater. Many more went on, despite travail and interrupted formal education, to become important historians, sociologists, artists, lawyers, and scientists. Many became major participants in new social movements that burst out of the conformity of the '50s, on into the '60s and beyond.*

Did we realize and appreciate how much individual potential abounded among us? We did appreciate each other, genuinely, but I did not begin to guess how much talent was budding there.

My age, thirty-four, made me a "graduate" of LYL early in 1956. Other factors ended my membership in the Communist Party in the summer of the same year. For a few months after LYL, my lot was to work directly with Eugene Dennis, General Secretary of the Communist Party. He had just returned from a long Smith Act jail term. I was, and had been for several years, an unofficial (that is, not publicly named) member of the National Board of the CP. Now I would briefly provide almost daily liaison between Dennis and William Z. Foster, the ailing National Chairman of the Party. That assignment handed me one of my unhappiest experiences. In April, 1956, Dennis became privy to the full, unpublished excoriation of Stalin's regime by Nikita Khrushchev at the Twentieth Congress of the Soviet Communist Party. He quickly gave it to me to read, then to bring to Foster, and no one else.

Others have described the shattering pain that document produced for those of us who never believed the horror tales until they finally came from the Soviet source. Actually I had begun to suspect a bit of the truth, but not its dimensions, from numerous press reports of rumored revelations in the Khrushchev speech. That was hardly preparation for the real thing. To stretch the anguish, I was the one who read the report aloud, word for searing word, to some hundred Party

---

* Robert Fogel, one of the last national leaders of LYL, changed course abruptly without apparent nostalgia, and his new academic career has taken him to the Nobel Prize in Economics for 1993.

leaders at an enlarged meeting of the National Committee later in April.

The Khrushchev report was the most powerful catalyst for the rethinking I began to do in 1956, but its terrible truths were not directly what made me leave the Party shortly afterward. Awakening to the reality of Stalinism did not terminate the cause of socialism for me, nor has the trauma of more recent disasters. There were Communist parties in other countries that, after 1956, drastically revised their historic view of "really existing socialism" in the USSR. They rejected notions of fealty to an ideological Mecca, and continued to champion socialism and the struggles of working people. Moreover, prospects for democratic reform of the Soviet system itself seemed to be opening up in the Khrushchev era. In the United States, however, the Communist Party had already become very weak, and the shock of a previously unaccepted reality was devastating. None of the antagonistic factions that responded in differing ways to the crisis appealed to me. I came to feel that the CPUSA, however altered, could not be the key to an eventually effective movement for radical social change.

Later in this manuscript, I will talk about the further evolution of my thinking, the flux of ideas and the questions that pursue anyone with visions of a more decent society. For now, I will say that I quit the Communist Party because its internal battles and frustrations were leading to a dead-end. My commitment to socialism and socialist movements was no longer tied to confidence in a self-anointed "vanguard." A significant movement had to be varied, pluralistic.

Roz and I decided to move our family to my home town, New Haven. We wanted to remake connections with work and people. I remember a long walk and talk with my brother just before we left New York. My hope was that before many years our family's ability to contribute to social movements would grow—and that could not happen if we allowed ourselves to be paralyzed by old habits, doctrines, and sectarian loyalties.

CHAPTER 2

SECOND TIME AROUND

Coming home to New Haven was beginning again. In this evolving new life, my family was the only constant, although the changes were big for each of us. Roz got a job first. Now *she* was the youth organizer, in charge of activities for children and youth at the New Haven Jewish Community Center. With a tip from an old friend, I soon found a semi-skilled job in a laboratory at the Armstrong Rubber factory.

We were gone from New York, but the FBI quickly let us know we were not forgotten. I was confronted by pairs of agents repeatedly on the Armstrong parking lot as I left work. They were delivering the message that my new job was fragile. This my boss confirmed, telling me that, because of Armstrong's defense contracts, I could stay on only if I didn't become a "public issue."

Despite the tensions, New Haven provided us the warmth and support we needed. There were old friends from my high school days, and, especially, new friends surrounding Roz at the Center. They knew what we were about, and shared a common aversion to McCarthyism. Of course, McCarthy had taken a great fall in 1954. McCarthyism was becoming a dirty word, even though its substance in our culture preceded McCarthy and survives him.

To some extent though, given the political probation imposed on my job at Armstrong, I was living under house arrest during our first year in New Haven. To break out, we decided that I had to set about building a career that seemed socially useful, without worrying about potential problems. The choice was to try to become a teacher, a big gamble in view of my previous political work. To prepare and qualify for a credential, I took night classes at Bridgeport University while working at Armstrong. Landing a public school job seemed unlikely, but one did come my way in the fall of 1957. A school superintendent, who told me he had once been a LaFollette liberal in Wisconsin, took the chance. He said it was time North Branford, a rural town near New Haven, hired an "atypical" teacher. He was referring to me not only as a radical, but as the only "non gentile" teacher.

The superintendent may or may not have considered the public consequences of his unorthodox decision. Roz and I were quite sure that this would become an issue. For better, we hoped, not for worse, it would blow the lid off an unnatural period of caution about what I could or couldn't say or do. For just five weeks beyond Labor Day, 1957, I had the most hectic job of my life, teaching all science and math classes for seventh, eighth, and ninth graders in North Branford Junior High School.

An election for the town's School Board, set for the first Tuesday in October, lit the fuse. First, the head of the local Taxpayers' Association declared war, pulling his daughter out of the "Commie" teacher's classes. The Democratic opposition made me the sole issue in their all-out campaign to unseat the Republican incumbents. They covered the town with leaflets reproducing an old *New York Times* report of my removal from the hearing of the House UnAmerican Activities Committee. They brought McCarthyism back in North Branford, with sound trucks, house-to-house canvassers, and phoned threats in the middle of the night to incumbent candidates' homes.

The weekend before the voting, police surrounded the school and the old School Board laid me off "for your own protection." Then strange things happened. The New Haven newspapers called what was happening to me politically motivated, in fact, McCarthyism. The junior high school students circulated petitions supporting me. The big surprise was the election result, an overwhelming rebuff for all the opposition candidates. But the School Board decided that I should not return to my job. The Town Counsel quipped at a public hearing that it had nothing to do with "Sputnik," which the Soviet Union had just put into orbit. It was only that, with my State teaching credential still being processed, I could be discharged without cause. Keeping me as a teacher was unnecessary and too much trouble.

The local American Civil Liberties Union persuaded me to go to court. A young Republican lawyer, whom we had just met socially, volunteered to represent me. For the next couple of months this was a front page story, with the community generally supportive to Roz at the Center and to Carla and David in their schools. This gave me the opportunity to establish my identity publicly in a way that was honest and comfortable. In a public letter, I was able to counter any notion that I apologized for my beliefs and values, past or present. I remained a socialist, unaffiliated. The ACLU accepted this, but the Connecticut Education Association did not. The CEA remained silent on the case because I refused to endorse their bylaw declaring that Communists should not have the right to be teachers.

North Branford finally agreed to our demand for public acknowledgment that I had not misrepresented myself at any time, and that the Board had no fault to find with my teaching.

They also agreed to give me back pay for time lost, a small sum indeed since my contract called for an annual salary of $3600.

We, and everyone we knew, felt very good about the outcome. No more walking on eggs! Still, I had to reconsider what to do for a living. There were no job offers, and it would be three months before something turned up. A suggestion that I could peddle encyclopedias was very depressing.

I was turned down for a technician's job at the Sterling Chemistry Laboratories of Yale University, but the interview led a few days later to an unexpected proposition. The Chair of Yale's Chemistry Department, who was also Chair of the local ACLU, phoned to ask if I would consider an opportunity to qualify for enrollment in the Ph.D. program in chemistry. The offer was a temporary technician's job, conditional on succeeding in some advanced undergraduate courses and then passing the graduate entrance examination in chemistry. I was scared. Over fifteen years had gone by since CCNY, and in the interval I never thought about going on in chemistry or any other graduate field. In fact, I would have felt less uncomfortable with an opportunity in a social science or literary field rather than in a hard science.

We decided the answer could only be yes, and my career in science began.

The first phase went quite well and I was admitted to the graduate program at Yale in September 1958. I began work with Harold Cassidy, an organic polymer chemist. I was involved in his collaboration with Jon Singer, a physical chemist who was studying protein molecules, especially antibodies and the immune system. The immune system became the focus of my research from that point on.

Although there were times when I thought I should bow to inevitable failure, neither Cassidy nor Singer ever seemed ready to give up on me. My biggest trouble was with Yale's monthly "cumulative exams" on unannounced, random topics in organic chemistry. I was not as flexible as Yale's younger students, inhibited by fears of exposing my confusion on an exam paper to a professor who might be my junior. I remember once when I came home in despair from a "cum." To cheer me up, Roz took me to the movies. The picture was Ingmar Bergman's *Wild Strawberries,* and its mood, especially the brutal scene of a professor browbeating a student, almost finished me. About my only escape from the "cum" ordeal came in strenuous basketball competition every Thursday night in the Adult League at the Jewish Community Center. Finally, before the deadline, I passed the magic number of nine "cums" required for advancement to Ph.D. candidacy.

Everything else proceeded far better than anticipated, and I got my Ph.D. in 1961. My thesis research led me to an idea I wanted to pursue in post doctoral work. The idea sounded good to Jon Singer, and he invited me to join him as a fellow when he accepted a professorship in the Biology Department of the new University of California campus at La Jolla. In August, 1961, our family moved to San Diego, California.

The transition to science, especially my time as a graduate student, was almost all consuming. Yet contact with the outside world of politics and culture continued. A memorable moment while we were still in New Haven was the opening of *Raisin in the Sun* at the Schubert Theater. Opening night was celebrated in our home with Lorraine Hansberry, Bob Nemiroff, and two other friends who were understudies in *Raisin,* Doug Ward and Lonnie Elder. There was a steady flow of old comrades and new acquaintances in our home, an unending exchange of political arguments about current and past events. This continued in San Diego, largely with colleagues at the new UC La Jolla campus. Roz, who again was youth activities director in a community center, brought us both into local activity around the first civil rights marches to take place in San Diego. We brought friends from San Diego's African-American community to campus to gain support for the civil rights movement.

Although my new career had begun more by chance and necessity than by choice, the science became deeply fascinating. A historic revolution was gaining strength in biology, and the cadre founding the La Jolla campus was enthusiastically attuned to it. At the center of the revolution was the rise of molecular genetics. The chemical composition and the structure of genes, and related polynucleotides, were rapidly being defined. The genetic code was being unraveled day by day in laboratories in several countries, so that it became possible to follow the pathways by which genetic information is passed along. Soon, important protein molecules, enzymes and antibodies, could be studied in connection with particular genes that determined for each a unique arrangement of chemical building blocks (amino acids).

The foundations had been laid in decades of research along many diverse lines, but suddenly connections were becoming clear. Previously separate fields of genetics, biochemistry, immunology, and cell biology were drawn together, each nourishing the other. Many young M.D.'s were attracted to work with Ph.D.'s in laboratories of molecular and cell biology. This transformation and integration of biological science would, within fifteen to twenty years, open the way to an explosive era of biotechnology and "genetic engineering."

My scientific preoccupation during thesis work at Yale and, more so, at La Jolla was with the central issue in immunology, the riddle of antibody specificity. A remarkable feature of the immune system is its capacity for discriminating between an almost limitless number of molecular displays (antigens). Antigens present themselves on the surfaces of bacteria, viruses, and all kinds of cells. If an antigen appears foreign to the host, its immune response produces antibodies and cells against that antigen. Singer and I, and many other researchers, wanted to know the make-up of the active sites of antibody molecules: what was the chemical arrangement that provided such exquisite recognition and discrimination? The main objective for those of us who were chemists was to find a way to attach a chemical label to the recognition sites of antibodies. Then, we thought, these large protein molecules could be split apart systematically to discover which small portion carried the label.

The idea that came to me while I was a graduate student did indeed develop into a general method for labeling a variety of antibody active sites. I designed an experimental system to verify the theory, and, once work began in La Jolla, success was quick and unequivocal. Such satisfying results are rarely achieved on the first try, and I have never since enjoyed quite the same "Eureka!" moment. Working with Jon Singer, and joined later by Henry Metzger, we published the first paper on our method, which we called "affinity labeling." We went on to secure the first evidence that an active site is shaped by contact between variable regions of two separate units (chains) of the antibody molecule.

Our contribution got a lot of attention, and, over the years, many laboratories have found affinity labeling a fruitful approach to some significant research problems. In the next few years, however, I was to learn something about how science often progresses. Although our method led to useful insights into antibody structure, it could not solve the chemical riddle of antibody specificity. The immune system is much too complex to have surrendered its secrets to our simple, frontal assault. The decisive breakthroughs came from other, less obvious directions of genetic and medical research. Studies of myeloma proteins, derived from human or mouse cancers of the cell type involved in antibody production, changed everything. Myelomas became the most important area of mammalian genetic research, which ultimately unraveled the antibody puzzle. Genes for the diverse classes of antibody molecules (the immunoglobulin protein family) have been defined in complete chemical detail. So have the array of immunoglobulin proteins coded by those genes. Now we know precisely what two antibody molecules have in common, and just what small variations from one to another allow each to recognize different antigens.

The excitement of molecular biology made me think about the moats that, for most of us, separate the worlds of science, culture and politics. In my LYL life, I read newspapers avidly and thought of myself as well informed—but I never sensed that a revolution in scientific knowledge, with enormous implications for the future, was under way. On the other hand, La Jolla, in its days as a shining new UC campus, was its own idyllic world apart. The joys of discovery were God's gift to us. The lives of ordinary mortals intruded infrequently and weakly, an occasional breeze from the civil rights storm rising in the South, or the shock of the assassination of Jack Kennedy in Dallas. Something closer to reality would take shape when students arrived, but undergraduate education had not yet begun during our stay.

While La Jolla made me uncomfortable, perhaps it also lulled me. I was anxious to leave a life so isolated, but I was unprepared for what happened when I began in 1963 to look elsewhere for an academic position. Because of affinity labeling, offers were numerous. What seemed the best was an Associate Professorship with tenure at the State University of New York at Buffalo. After returning from a visit to Buffalo, where I passed through the usual academic recruiting ritual of seminars, wining and dining, I accepted the offer. The Dean of Biology responded with delight, asking me to fill out the required employment forms and "pop them back" in the mail. One of the forms was based on the Feinberg Law, New York's version of the loyalty oaths imposed on teachers and other public employees by almost every state legislature during the McCarthy hysteria. These loyalty oaths, like the Smith and McCarran acts, would in the next few years be ruled unconstitutional by the Supreme Court—but not until they robbed many people of their jobs.

The Feinberg Law was so bad, it is hard to believe it was ever tolerated and enforced. With the form I got from Buffalo, there was an official New York State pamphlet telling me the "rules and regulations" in detail. First, if I had ever been a member of any of two hundred plus organizations on the US Attorney General's "subversive" list, I was required to disclose this to the Chancellor. Moreover, every department chairman was required to submit annual reports to superiors, ultimately to the Chancellor, of any subversive "words or deeds" by any member of the department faculty, whether in the classroom or anywhere else.

I wrote to Chancellor Furnas. The Feinberg Law was outrageous and unconstitutional. Under protest, I affirmed that I had indeed belonged to organizations on the Attorney General's list. When I assumed my position in Buffalo, I would work hard to overturn the law, which surely was opposed by the vast majority of public school teachers and other public employees.

Furnas never replied. A chagrined Dean told me the job offer was vetoed.

My immunology colleagues around the country were astonished and angry. More job invitations appeared. One was from the University of Pittsburgh, where I was assured that what occurred in New York "couldn't happen here." Pittsburgh was a private university, not a state institution.

Roz and I were both invited to look Pittsburgh over. The days we spent there were not at all the usual recruiting ritual. Everything was done to show us that Pittsburgh was different. Molly Yard was running for local office, and we were brought together socially with progressive, feminist leaders of her campaign. We were taken to a festival of music and dance that displayed Pittsburgh's rich endowment of national group cultures. There was, of course, science as well, especially many hours spent with future Nobel Laureate Niels Jerne, one of immunology's greatest minds. (Jerne's presence on the faculty was one of Pittsburgh's major attractions for me, but there was no hint that he was soon to leave for a prestigious position in Europe.)

When I received Pittsburgh's formal offer, which included a big start-up grant for my research, I accepted. Roz gave notice on her job, and we were all ready to go. Some time later, I was invited to consider an appointment in UC Berkeley's Department of Bacteriology and Immunology. While I would have preferred Berkeley, I was already committed to Pittsburgh. I could look at Berkeley only if Pittsburgh unexpectedly reneged at the last moment.

Again strange things happened. Instead of sending me a contract to sign, Pittsburgh fell silent as weeks went by. Roger Stanier, Berkeley's leading bacteriologist, decided to phone the Chair of Pittsburgh's Biology Department. He found a deeply depressed Ellis Englesberg, a former student of Stanier's. He said the Board of Trustees had decided to stop my appointment, and that his Dean was going to send me an ambiguous letter aimed at avoiding a possible law suit. The Dean's letter came soon after. He told me, for my "own protection," that if I came to Pittsburgh, I could not expect the award of tenure after my first year as Associate Professor. Regretfully, he said, my position would be terminated at that point because the Trustees could not risk the loss of financial support resulting from a politically controversial appointment. The problem, according to the Dean, was the Pennsylvania loyalty law, which required annual reports on "subversives" employed by a private institution if it receives any state funds.

I wrote back that Roz and I liked Pittsburgh, and that we would come anyway. We would take our chances on next year. The Dean's reply, as expected, dropped the subterfuge and withdrew the offer altogether.

The year was now 1964, ten years after McCarthy's personal Waterloo, but the "loyalty" saga was not over. California's loyalty oath had already been modified sharply after years of campus turmoil. The UC Regents, however, still had veto power (later relinquished) over faculty appointments. When the academic review process was complete, the UC campus agreed to my appointment as Associate Professor with tenure. Again trustees, this time the Regents, held up the appointment. Instead of going to Berkeley in July as planned, we were in limbo again.

However, this time was the charm. Leading professors at UC Berkeley and UC San Diego intervened strongly. Jon Singer and Harold Urey wrote to UC President Clark Kerr that if an academically approved appointment could be overturned on political grounds, they would reconsider their place in the University. The Regents stepped aside, and, in August, 1964, Berkeley became our home.

A postscript should be noted here. The chairpersons of both departments where I almost went, Buffalo and Pittsburgh, protested the violation of academic freedom and soon left their campuses in disgust. The late Bernard Baker, an organic chemist who had done pioneering work analogous to affinity labeling, moved to UC Santa Barbara. So, coincidentally, did Ellis Englesberg.

CHAPTER 3

INTO THE SIXTIES

Both my parents died, within six weeks of each other, very soon after Roz and I came to Berkeley. For their last few illness-racked months of life, they were cared for by Malcolm and his family in Hartford, Connecticut.

My parents had moved to New York in 1944, where my father continued as a Communist Party worker until his death. I was always close to both parents, and we gave each other support and companionship during insecure times. My mother was in poor health and seriously incapacitated during most of the New York years. Clare was always the family's mainstay in dealing with health and other problems of living in the big city.

When I left the Party in 1956, my father understood and supported my decision. Our reactions to the Khrushchev disclosures about Stalin and Stalinism were the same. He also saw the Party's futile state of isolation, narrowness, internal feuding and progressive disintegration. He felt, though, that he was too old to gamble on a personal search for new directions. His unhappiness about what was happening was fueled by earlier disheartening experiences with an undemocratic Party structure and some hardened bureaucrats. Yet his disappointment was mitigated by his pride in the Party's history of struggle for social justice and an abiding faith in the inevitability of human progress toward socialism.

The day before he died, my brother read him the headline in the *New York Times* announcing the downfall of Nikita Khrushchev. In intolerable pain and barely able to speak, he took the news as a hopeful sign that the Soviet Union and China were ready to bury the hatchet. Watch, he whispered, Mao will leave too—it's part of an arrangement to restore unity. In his last days, he was also preoccupied with Barry Goldwater's war mongering presidential campaign, and his final political act was to vote by absentee ballot for Lyndon Johnson.

Now it is a comfort to know that he can't come back like Rip Van Winkle to see what became of his fondest hopes, so far anyway.

Life turned around for each member of the family when we moved to Berkeley. David was starting his freshman year at Harvard. Carla, who had been away in college for three years, was at UC Berkeley and lived at home with us for her senior year. Several months after our arrival, Roz started what was to be her most important and satisfying job.

Roz became chief coordinator of services for developmentally disabled children and adults in Contra Costa County. She headed a community council formed by parents of the disabled, and although financial support came from the County, she was largely independent of governmental bureaucracies. Roz and the Council were in at the beginning of a period of growing consciousness about the needs of persons with mental retardation, cerebral palsy, autism and other disabilities appearing at birth or early childhood. This was sparked in part because attention was called to the problem by President Kennedy, whose sister was born with mental retardation. Roz would spend the next twenty years as a leader in this movement. The Developmental Disabilities Councils in the East Bay became a model of effective community action for rights and services, and against discrimination or callous neglect. Their advances foreshadowed the general uprising of disabled people that took off independently in Berkeley and that led, after militant national actions, to the enactment of the landmark Americans With Disabilities Act.

For me, UC Berkeley was a brand new universe of intellectual and social experience. Here, only the unexpected was commonplace. If La Jolla felt removed from the real world, Berkeley was soon so connected with social issues that it often seemed unreal in quite a different way. It was churning over problems that most of the country was slow even to perceive.

My initiation to academic responsibility was abrupt and demanding. As was the custom in those days, my teaching assignment in the first year was light so that I could set up my laboratory and write applications for grants to support my research program. However, the Bacteriology and Immunology Department at Berkeley was not a happy place in 1964. Most veteran members of the Bacteriology faculty were not on speaking terms with the old time Immunology professors. Both sides courted the two new Immunology faculty members, and we felt trapped. The bacteriologists were close conceptually, and in personal relationships, with the international network of pioneers in the new molecular biology. Their own outstanding research contributions were along lines more traditional than radical, but they did not respect the empirical and pragmatic research of the senior immunologists, the lack of logical theory and "hard" science.

The feud had actually begun early in the Cold War, when the most prominent bacteriologist, Roger Stanier, condemned the participation of some of the immunologists in the government's secret germ warfare research. During the McCarthy period, one of the immunologists, Charles Kreuger, who was a Naval officer, retaliated by charging Stanier's closest colleague, Professor Michael Dudoroff, with making derogatory remarks about the Korean War—and the latter was denied federal research support for several years.

Since I was then ignorant of the background of the feud, and on speaking terms with all of the active faculty (Kreuger had retired), the job of negotiating a reorganization of the department fell to me. The resolution of the conflict, agreed to by both sides, was for the older immunologists to leave the department and form a new medical microbiology group in the School of Public Health. The professors remaining in our department (later renamed the Department of Microbiology and Immunology) got along well. More than in most departments, our faculty, students, and staff were able to relate to each other, and these relations actually improved in the campus upheaval that was soon to begin with the Free Speech Movement (FSM).

When I consider how to tell about my years at UC Berkeley, I feel as if I'm dealing with three lives, concurrent and interwoven. There was my scientific life in immunology, my academic and teaching activity, and my involvement in social movements during the tempestuous 1960s and after. I think I have to start with the last, because events that erupted two months after my arrival on campus ruled out any orderly sequence of adjustment to new circumstances. My life had never been this complicated. Before there was always a clear focus of primary responsibility, whether as a radical youth organizer, a graduate student, or a post-doctoral researcher. It turned out that the blend of science, of teaching and academic duties, and of social and political involvement made each of these endeavors far more difficult than any one of them had been in the past. My life in the McCarthy period seemed simple in comparison.

Perhaps I can merge my personal experience of the 1960s with a retrospective view of how the faculty at UC participated in and was buffeted by the remarkable events of that decade. The starting point of the story, the birth of FSM in October 1964, has been retold many times. The Chancellor of the Berkeley campus reacted to growing student protests against Jim Crow establishments and practices in the Bay Area. He issued regulations that put a quarantine on political activity: the campus was not to be a "launching pad" for demonstrations in the community, and "outsiders" were banned from distributing leaflets on campus. The surprise, however, was that students refused to obey and boldly violated the new rules. Quite a few were fresh from an inspiring summer as freedom riders and voter registration workers in the South, and a whole generation was about to break the silence of conformity that smothered dissent in the 1950s. When police tried to arrest a leaflet distributor on Sproul Plaza, the police car was surrounded by hundreds and eventually thousands. Civil disobedience had come to the Berkeley campus and the FSM was underway.

My window on FSM and the events that followed for the next eight years led to an article I wrote in 1984. It was requested by the Graduate Student Assembly, UCB, in observance of the FSM's twentieth anniversary. I include it here as a description of how I remember those years and what they meant to me:

WHERE WERE YOU, GRANDPA,
DURING BERKELEY'S GREAT WARS?

I joined the faculty at Berkeley in August, 1964—just two months before the great free speech rebellion began. Coincidence? Not according to the Thirteenth Report of the (California) Senate Factfinding Subcommittee on Un-American Activities, June, 1965.

I arrived on campus as newly appointed Associate Professor in the Department of Bacteriology and Immunology, but the Un-American Committee headed by State Senator Hugh Burns saw through that ruse. With vintage McCarthyite vision, it insisted that my communist background and radical organizing experience as a youth were what really brought me here. So before I ever met Mario Savio, or any of the student leaders who launched the FSM, the Burns Committee gave me a major share of the credit for their remarkable success.

Now, twenty years after the FSM and I came to Berkeley, I'd like to look back a bit at how some of us on the faculty related to the student upheavals of the Sixties: FSM, the Vietnam War, People's Park, the Third World Strike, et al. This has remained an untold story. That fact is strange in a way, since the UC faculty was a prime target during those years for the finger-pointing press and politicians, especially when Ronald Reagan took over as Governor. On the other hand, the story of the Sixties is youth's rebellion, and many of the histories of that period were written by members of the generation that coined the phrase, "Don't trust anyone over thirty."

FSM

From the beginning on October 1, 1964, when the police car was surrounded on Sproul Plaza, a few faculty immediately were sympathetic to the students. They were upset at the spectacle of a police action ordered by Chancellor Strong to prevent political speech and activity on Sproul Plaza. Philosophy Professor John Searle went right to the scene of the incident and spoke up against the Administration's restriction of free speech. In the following weeks, as the impasse with Strong continued and concern grew, Searle was joined by other faculty members in frequent consultations. Among the most involved were two young assistant professors in the History Department, Reginald Zelnik and Lawrence Levine. In the Academic Senate, Levine was treated as an upstart when he tried to get that body to intervene in favor of a more democratic policy toward student activities.

The faculty as a whole did not respond to what was happening until the sit-in and mass arrests at Sproul Hall at the beginning of December. Outrage over the Administration's resort to massive police intervention and the Chancellor's unwillingness to give an inch on elementary issues of civil liberties brought 800 faculty members together in an emergency meeting on the afternoon of December 3, the day that dawned with the student arrests. At that meeting, Roger Stanier of Bacteriology and Immunology read a telegram to Governor Brown protesting the arrests, which was endorsed in a motion passed by acclamation.

On the evening of the same day, there was a meeting of faculty who came to be known as the Committee of 200. Here it was agreed to draft a resolution for submission to the

Academic Senate embodying the essential free speech demands of the students. For the next several years, although the Committee of 200 had no formal existence as an organization, faculty who took part in that initial effort continued to cooperate and became the most significant influence in the Academic Senate. Some of the original participants left the fold at one time or another and new ones joined.

Even after the sit-in arrests, most faculty expected that President Clark Kerr would be able to accomplish what Chancellor Strong would not. The faculty had great respect for Kerr's credentials as a liberal highly skilled in educational diplomacy and the art of compromise. However, the illusion that Kerr could bring about a return to normalcy died in the Greek Theatre fiasco of December 7, when Mario Savio's attempt to speak in reply to Kerr was throttled by police who dragged him off the platform. On the next day, December 8, the Academic Senate rebuffed the Administration and passed the resolution of the Committee of 200 by an astonishing vote of 824 to 115.

I have a very personal recollection of December 7th and 8th, 1964. A short time after the Greek Theatre episode, I got an urgent message from a veteran faculty member who was very close to the Administration. I was to go at once to see the Acting Chancellor, who had been asked by Clark Kerr to seek my advice. Edward Strong was no longer functioning as Chancellor although this was a secret even to the faculty, as was the identity of his temporary replacement. Whenever I think back to my memorable interview with the Acting Chancellor, I am amused and embarrassed. I felt flattered and so hopeful as I gave my advice for transmission to Clark Kerr. After the Greek Theatre, I thought, the Administration is at last opening its mind to the need for reaching a serious agreement with the students. My advice was that the Administration should make an unequivocal act of good faith by giving its support to the resolution of the Committee of 200 at the next day's Academic Senate meeting. That night my wife and I dropped in on the faculty member who had asked me to meet with the Acting Chancellor so that we could give him the good news. His mood was in sombre contrast to my elation. "Leon," he said, "you have disappointed us." He said I had been called in because "we" (the Administration) didn't have the experience for coping with Mario Savio and his friends who "talk the language of the gutter... We thought that with your background, you would know how to handle them." Of course, my wife and I immediately walked out. (I resist the temptation to reproduce my angry rejoinder as we went for the door.)

The sequel to this little story came years later, when I got some of my FBI files under the Freedom of Information Act. Although only the Acting Chancellor and I had been in the room during our conversation on December 7, 1964, an FBI file carried the report of that encounter taking note of my very unwelcome advice.

Far from sharing the Administration's hostility toward the FSM leaders, many faculty saw something admirable in the new students of the Sixties. Although often discomfited by the unprecedented disruption of the norms of academia, faculty sympathetic to FSM were struck by the idealism and honesty of a new generation that got its inspiration through direct participation in the historic civil rights movement. They found Mario Savio an especially attractive representative of the new student, so different from the Silent Generation of the Fifties. His speech was forthright and fresh, without the clichés that would have permitted smug academics to dismiss him as an "ideologue." He and other FSM leaders were perceptive and devastatingly candid about platitudes and hypocrisy that are part of standard operating procedure in all big establishments, including the university.

Some faculty in the Committee of 200 had themselves taken part in civil rights actions, for example in San Francisco's "auto row." The bond for others was a strong commitment to civil liberties and academic freedom, expressed earlier in their refusal to submit to the Leavering "loyalty oath" imposed on the university during the years of McCarthyism.

In fact, in the Fall of 1964, a very major academic freedom fight was going forward against the firing of Assistant Professor of German, Eli Katz, for his refusal to answer questions put to him first by the House Committee on Un-American Activities and later by Chancellor Strong. In November, 1964, the Academic Senate voted 267 to 79 to insist that Katz be reinstated. That fight, which eventually was won, was led by Howard Schachman of Molecular Biology, who became one of the most effective leaders of the Committee of 200, and by the late Jacobus tenBroek of Political Science. (Professor tenBroek is celebrated for his brilliant legal analysis of violations of the U.S. Constitution involved in the internment of Japanese-Americans during World War II.)

I will save for later some reflections on shifts in attitudes of groups of faculty as the varied battles of the Sixties evolved. The FSM projected a spirit that was to influence the flow of events for the remainder of the Sixties, and beyond, not only at Berkeley, but nationwide and even worldwide. What it accomplished and what it didn't, its impact on students and on faculty, on the university and on the outside world, can be estimated only from an overview of all that followed in its wake.

My own relationship to the FSM and what followed was shaped by several things. As my FBI files reveal, my past— especially as main spokesperson of the Labor Youth League from 1949 to 1956—made me a prime target for one of the FBI's "CoIntelPro" campaigns. Before I taught my first class in immunology, the FBI warned Governor Edmund Brown of my presence. While I was overwhelmed with the normal jitters of setting up teaching and research programs in a new and, to me, rather awe-inspiring faculty position, the FBI was feeding material to a Birch Society journal of the period called *Tocsin*, and to then Congressman Mulford so that they could "discredit" me. Actually it was the Burns (Un-American Committee) Report, published eight months after the birth of FSM, that led to my first acquaintance with any of the major student leaders. A few individuals were impressed by my response to the Committee, published in the *San Francisco Chronicle*, and sought me out to express their support. Bettina Aptheker became a good friend as did, later still, Mario Savio and quite a few other student activists.

From the beginning, I was very interested in the reactions of faculty and administration to the student "unrest." My strong predisposition was that the students should be heard and treated with respect. Like many of my colleagues, I was totally opposed to attempts to turn off the demands and concerns of the students by ultimatum and police force. Even though I was new to the club, I could not refrain from taking the floor at Academic Senate meetings, especially as patterns of police action and, eventually, National Guard intervention became more frequent through those turbulent times.

Some of the Academic Senate meetings were memorable, especially those called in emergencies. There is such a thing as an academic style, albeit the forms are diverse, which I often admired, but never could claim for myself. I remember the wry humor of English Professor Tom Parkinson, the satirical quality of the late David Krech of Psychology, the parliamentary astuteness of Frank Newman of Law and Charles Sellers of History. I felt somehow like an immigrant in a new world when I spoke directly and with some passion, which was true to my own background and values, but quite strange in the company of scholars. The difference was more of spirit than substance, since other colleagues felt the issues of the time as deeply as I did.

AGAINST THE VIETNAM WAR

While FSM focused on student rights and educational reform, it was Berkeley's early and continuous massive protests against the Vietnam War that turned attention to society as a whole. The anti-establishment mood erupted into broader arenas of challenge to the war, to prevailing cultural norms and social institutions, to oppression of racial minorities and the Third World. Over the next several years, the chain of student and youth rebellions initiated in 1964 extended to virtually every U.S. campus, as well as to Paris, Rome, Tokyo, Prague, and numerous other world centers.

At Berkeley, several faculty members joined students in the earliest protests against the Vietnam War. Steve Smale of Mathematics was part of the direct actions blocking the passage of troop trains. The first teach-ins were held despite an attempted ban by the Alameda County Board of Supervisors. In 1965, the Faculty Peace Committee (FPC) was formed. That Committee met almost weekly when the university was in session and was active through the remaining years of the Vietnam War. Franz Schurmann of Sociology and History,

Peter Scott of English, and Reginald Zelnik of History wrote *The Politics of Escalation*, one of the first and most convincing books indicting U.S. policy in Vietnam.

The Faculty Peace Committee was a rather unique outfit by standards of the Sixties. It was non-parochial in its interests, pluralistic in its encouragement of the different, sometimes competing, approaches to developing peace movements and strategies. Its weekly bull sessions were exchanges of opinion and analysis of world events and local issues. It developed its own projects, supported participation in many others, and generally avoided issuing pronouncements on the "rights" and "wrongs" of the tactics of other peace groups. As a result, it was essentially free of the kinds of pulling and tearing that grew with the mounting frustrations of the peace movement as the Vietnam War wore on.

Of course, there was no escaping some of the skirmishes on the Left. Some of us who took part in the big anti-war marches joined with student leaders to defeat Jerry Rubin's dangerous proposal to crash the police lines that barred entry to Oakland. Several of our major projects were in turn attacked by some as "liberal" diversions from more militant encounters.

One Faculty Peace Committee highlight was the great public debate on the Vietnam War between Arthur Goldberg, U.S. Ambassador to the United Nations, and Franz Schurmann for the FPC. It was held on March 25, 1966, before thousands in a packed Harmon Gym, with loud speakers set up outside for an additional couple of thousand students and faculty. Goldberg had been invited to receive an honorary degree on Charter Day, which aroused strong campus protest. The debate, unprecedented in that it directly involved a high level spokesman of the Johnson Administration, completely overshadowed the degree-granting ritual performed earlier in the Greek Theatre. Despite the tension surrounding the event, and the provocative quality of the Ambassador's pro war argument, the huge crowd held back its response until after the vote that Reggie Zelnik, who presided, said would take place. Then Goldberg was given a message to take back to Johnson: a vote by the assemblage of about 7000, with no more than a score on the other side, to condemn the war and government policy in Vietnam. The noise that followed was monumental as every voice was raised to give emphasis to the message.

The Vietnam Commencement, convened on May 17, 1968 by the Campus Draft Opposition, was as large and impressive a ceremony as the Berkeley campus has seen. Seven hundred and seventy three draft eligible UC students, many of them graduating seniors, took a public oath declaring: "Our war in Vietnam is unjust and immoral. As long as the United States is involved in this war I will not serve in the Armed Forces." About eight thousand students and faculty gathered in Sproul Plaza to honor and support them in the face of a Regents' ban on the observance. I was chosen to chair the program, which included Robert Hutchins as the featured "Commencement" speaker. On the eve of the "illegal" gathering, Governor Reagan demanded that disciplinary action be instituted against any faculty who participated. The response of three hundred members of the faculty was to publicly endorse the ceremony and to stand together on the steps of Sproul Hall during the proceedings. This was one of the rare occasions when Reagan and the Regents backed down, and no punitive action followed.

The Campus Draft Opposition was perhaps the most notable example of unified commitment and very warm relationships between student and faculty peace activists.

A PEOPLE'S PARK TALE

I will not try to describe faculty involvement with students in projects of which I was not a part. Quite a few faculty were enthusiastic backers of People's Park, which was created on an unused, run down plot of UC-owned land taken over by student and community activists. While not unsympathetic to those who, in the late Sixties, tried to create islands of freedom from dominant cultural and institutional controls, I was not swept up in the excitement and symbolism of People's Park.

In the end, though, no one on the Berkeley campus could escape the ramifications of People's Park. Buckshot fired by massed police, tear gas released from swooping helicopters, National Guard bayonets surrounding the campus on orders of Governor Reagan—all of this left no sanctuary for a passive observer. One person was killed and another blinded by· police fire. With the National Guard out in full force, Berkeley was close to becoming what Kent State became one year later.

In this setting, on May 21, 1969, seventeen professors took off for Sacramento to see if we could prevail on Republican and Democratic legislators to use their influence to get the Guard called off and reduce the risk of greater tragedy. We took our peace mission very seriously, did not seek publicity that might jeopardize our effort, and did not ask to see the Governor so as not to chance an inflammatory confrontation.

Governor Reagan, however, had a different agenda. As we talked with individual legislators, and felt we were making headway, a message came that the Governor wanted to see us. At the small auditorium to which we were summoned, we entered into a media event. Television cameras from all of the networks and dozens of reporters were there.

Then Ronald Reagan came in and strode to the podium. His face was rouged, made up for the cameras which flashed on his presence.

Nobel Laureate Owen Chamberlain spoke for us and quietly began to tell the Governor why we had come. He got no further along than a sentence or two when the Governor took over. Waving a pointed finger at us, he declared that "you professors" are responsible for all the violence, "you" told your students that they could break the law. Reagan went on, lecturing and accusing the egg heads for the benefit of the evening TV news and the morning headlines.

Here, my story of that day becomes more personal. Fearing that our mission was ending in disaster, nothing more than a propaganda coup for the Governor, I interrupted the monologue. I said something like, "That's a fine political speech, Governor, but we came here to talk reason, to see what can be done to avoid further violence." I won't try to reproduce here the back and forth debate of the next fifteen or so minutes. Thanks to the Governor, it was all captured on TV by eager crews who were unabashedly delighted by the rare unstaged drama. Reagan demanded at once to know "who are you?", then said he knew my name well and wouldn't be surprised at anything I said.

When I said that the Governor was responsible for the atmosphere of intimidation, for trying to run the campus by bayonet, for firing and threatening to fire any university administrator who might be willing to negotiate, the Governor exploded with rage and shouted "liar." (Over the next few days reports were given to the press again about my political background, but the late Charles McCabe wrote in his *Chronicle* column: "Whatever Mr. Wofsy's background, or foreground, his question was proper, and his charge correct.")

Our conference with Reagan ended when Owen Chamberlain said that if the Governor persisted he would earn a reputation on California's campuses like Lyndon Johnson's in Vietnam. With that, Reagan spun around and stalked out.

That whole scene inevitably received a great deal of publicity, worldwide, not as one of the sterling media performances for which President Reagan is today famous. I hope the reader will forgive me for indulging in this story after fifteen years and wanting my grandchildren to be able to read about it. I offer it not as history, but as a savored memory of the day I met the Great Communicator.

There is a little more, an aftermath to this encounter. My instant notoriety brought me a flood of letters. About half were congratulatory. The other half were hate mail, full of anti-Semitic and other racist vulgarity. There were death threats, including a funeral wreath. A paramilitary group wrote that it voted by a slim margin to permit me to finish out the semester, after which I would be terminated if I ever tried to teach again.

It has always struck me that both the hate and the fan letters were variations on a common theme, one strange and alarming in a democracy: How dare you (or how brave to) voice dissent in the presence of authority.

FACULTY SHIFTS

Hostility to student activism became more pronounced within the faculty as issues and grievances became more diverse, as the campus became more chaotic, and as the university came under intense economic and political fire especially from the Governor. An early milestone in this process occurred after Roger Heyns became Chancellor in 1966. He took into his administration a few of the faculty who had been critical of Strong and Kerr and supportive of FSM demands for educational reform.

I remember John Searle seeking opinions before he accepted a key post in the Chancellor's Office. The view I expressed was that he should take the job since his commitment to the students was strong, and the only good administrator would be one willing to resign if principle should require it. But the new administration bowed to outside pressure and called in the police to arrest students protesting the presence of a Navy recruiting booth on campus. No one resigned.

One crisis followed another in the next few years, crescendos of antagonism being reached over People's Park and, under still another Chancellor, the Third World Strike.

THIRD WORLD STRIKE

It is something worth pondering that the Third World Strike, and its demands for a college or school of Third World studies, probably aroused deeper feelings of opposition among faculty than any other significant campus movement of the time. Nor did it receive impressive support from most of the student body. This is somewhat paradoxical: first, because the civil rights movement gave birth to the campus revolts of the Sixties, and, second, because the Third World Strike was one of the few struggles to achieve significant, though limited, academic changes (establishment of the Ethnic Studies departments).

The intensity of faculty hostility to the strike is explained only in part by its militancy and the fact that "trashing" sorties on and around campus were becoming a fashion at the time.

Charges of racism were rampant—for academics, this was especially hard to take. A small, but highly accomplished number of faculty were justly proud of their academic contributions in areas of history and sociology relevant to the experience of blacks and other minorities. They reacted against what they saw as a wave of anti-intellectualism. The bulk of the faculty, secure in its self-image as an elite by criteria of ethics as well as of intellect, saw its mission as defense of the academic citadel against the erosion of "excellence." The campus administration was actually a bit more sensitive than the faculty to the need for some positive gestures to meet legitimate criticism.

The Third World Strike, for all its harshness, was telling the university two truths which, to this day, it is unwilling to hear. One, the university is not an oasis of freedom from racism, but contributes at many levels to the barriers that alienate and largely exclude black and Latino youth. Two, that will never change without bold measures to establish a significant presence of minorities on the faculty and their involvement in shaping the academic environment.

I won't argue those points here, but I mention them because there was so little understanding and self-examination by faculty at the time of the Third World Strike. Nor is there evidence of more openness by today's faculty to any creative concept of affirmative action in the university.[*]

---

[*] Since this was written, two successive campus administrations have made headway in expanding enrollment of students of color, especially at the undergraduate level. Some faculty have participated actively, and several faculty members of color have spearheaded the effort. Many on the faculty remain unengaged or resistant to efforts to recruit minority faculty members and to develop multicultural academic programs. (February, 1994)

WHAT HAPPENED TO
EDUCATIONAL REFORM?

Beyond free speech, the thrust of FSM was for educational reform. The aim was to change the university, to humanize it and make it more democratic. The idea was to expand and elevate the faculty-student interaction, reducing the role of administration. (To make the point, Savio's rhetorical suggestion was that administration should concern itself with such tasks as keeping the floors swept clean.)

The students were very critical of faculty, the lack of interest of many in teaching, their political timidity and educational conservatism. Yet some faculty and students were able to form a very productive and warm relationship toward the end of the Sixties in thinking through serious programs for educational reform to recommend to the Academic Senate. The most significant contribution was the report, *The Culture of the University*, produced by a joint student and faculty Study Commission on University Governance.

The general mood of the faculty, however, was less and less favorable to reform as turbulence continued to shake the campus. One last big movement for change erupted when the university was "reconstituted" for a few days in the wake of Nixon's bombing of Cambodia at the end of 1972. Impatience with the university, and anger over its service to the military-industrial complex, merged with outrage over the expanding war. Once again, many thousands of students brought "business as usual" to a dramatic halt. A minority of faculty—with Sheldon Wolin of Political Science in the lead—worked with student leaders to develop constructive educational models that would make the university more vital in those difficult times.

The symbolic "reconstitution" was short-lived. Its aftermath was a determined and ultimately successful effort to restore faculty control to a traditionalist establishment. The Academic Senate was gutted by the formation of a so-called Representative Assembly. The Assembly was ineffectual except for its "dog in the manger" role, replacing general meetings of the faculty where significant debates and action used to occur. Even token participation of students on faculty committees is resisted, interdisciplinary and experimental educational programs have a harder time than ever making it through the administrative obstacle course.

So, What Did FSM Achieve?

Twenty years later the legacy of FSM is not to be found in an altered university, one more humane and democratic. True, the embarrassingly crude restrictions on free speech that triggered the rebellion were finally scrapped. But stopping the machine did not reform, let alone revolutionize the system.

Still, the worth of popular movements cannot be weighed on a scale of "cost effectiveness." Measured by programmatic goals attained, the palpable successes of most struggles for social change rarely match the ideals, energy and sacrifice invested.

The real successes of the FSM are larger by far than might appear from any analysis of university regulations and educational policy. Like the civil rights movement, FSM broke the pattern of passivity toward injustice at a very critical time in our national history. It wasn't an accident that Berkeley became the first major staging area of opposition to the Vietnam War that later swept the nation. That was the earliest affirmation of FSM.

FSM's spirit of challenge to authority also grew into a generational refusal to conform to society's more arbitrary, often hypocritical norms of behavior and human relationships. While the youth movements of the Sixties did not themselves overcome patterns of sexism, they provided impetus for the feminist groundswell that followed.

When some look back at the Sixties, especially those who may do so from a now more comfortable faculty perch, they tend to remember disorder, disrespect, emotionalism, inconvenience. But Berkeley was in significant ways more, not less, of a university at that time. Whatever confusion and even nonsense was in the air, we engaged issues, dealt with ideas and with each other as people across the territorial confines of particular academic disciplines.

Among society's institutions, universities are especially conflicted in their mission and make-up. They have a very important job to do for the prevailing society, a heavy obligation to provide the continuity that keeps the wheels of the system turning. But learning produces questioning of established ways, often beyond what may be acceptable notions for improving the workings of the machine. Moreover, the university functions by the continuous flow into its midst of new generations, those who are most prone (as the inherent quality of youth) to challenge the old and, periodically, to kick over the traces.

The faculty's professional and intellectual mission is not independent of society's expectations, its positive inducements as well as its negative pressures. The challenge of youth, however, exerts its own pressure, sometimes pushing ideas from purely intellectual to moral ground. That can infect faculty, and that's what the FSM did for a time for some of us.

FSM is history, but the phenomenon will show up again—not as pale repetition, but in the language and style of another generation that refuses to believe there is nothing new under the sun.

My reminiscence ends with a story. Recently, I sat in a room with several former leaders of FSM. They gathered in response to a request for cooperation by a young person who wanted to portray the FSM experience in a film. There certainly were pros and cons to consider, but they are beside the point here. Someone put into words one of the main dilemmas on the minds of most present: "Can we trust a kid to tell our story?"

That little anecdote doesn't carry a heavy moral, but I thought it was worth sharing.

CHAPTER 4

BERKELEY AFTER THE STORM

More than twenty years of teaching at Berkeley taught me some things I had only sensed as a parent. Roz and I had experienced crises with our own children, yet things never seemed impossible and intervals of worry and doubt were not long lasting. But Carla and David came through childhood and finished high school before the wild years of drugs, mystical tripping, and far out life styles. In the late Sixties and the Seventies, the best of our students were in personal turmoil, frustrated by social norms and authority they would not accept. Several were drawn to strange mixtures of science and superstition. I was angrily rebuked by two excellent graduate students because I took for granted that the astrological charts they were fashioning were simply a form of amusement. Some students tried (out of fondness for me, they said) to convince me how much insight into the immune system I would gain from smoking pot. One student, who went to live in an ashram for a time, told me that in her guru's powerful presence she could visualize in detail how her lymphocytes were interacting.

The remarkable thing, though, was that crises seemingly beyond resolution, mistakes that seemed to doom an individual, left no indelible imprint a few years later. A worthwhile, even admirable, human being could emerge from a temporarily lost and unreachable soul. It came home to me that choices everyone regards as enormously important in youth are often less than fateful or final. Almost nothing is irreversible if years are ahead. Probably in this observation is an element of rationalization—for the hardest thing I found as a teacher was to write off a student as a failure. I could and would tell a student what I thought, but I could not exercise my authority to close the case. Sometimes the long-term results transformed my indecisiveness into a virtue. Several of my students who once seemed hopelessly mixed up excel today in their own research and teaching (including the one who once endowed her guru with omniscience in immunology). In a few cases, though, the outcome proved I had cooperated in wasting the student's time and avoiding the need for a better choice.

Teaching in the classroom was a lot easier emotionally, though intellectually no less demanding, than guiding graduate students and postdoctoral fellows in research. For eight years, I taught the main graduate course in Immunology, and for another seven, the major undergraduate course. With the field leaping ahead, it was never a matter of passing on an established body of facts from one year to the next. Instead, I tried to focus on the development of ideas—perceptions shifting and questions reformulated under a tidal wave of experimental results. With scientific knowledge accumulating so rapidly, and fragmenting into myriad specialties, it is easy for new generations to lose the culture of a field, its roots in intellectual curiosity, conflicting theories and interpretations. I remember how exhilarating (and unusual) it was when an older organic chemistry prof at Yale took class time to read to us raging polemics from the nineteenth century over Kekule's proposed structure of the benzene ring.

My research program, supported without interruption by grants from the National Institutes of Health, moved gradually from antibody molecules to the study of lymphocytes, the cells that carry the properties of specific recognition and memory in an immune response. In 1972, Claudia Henry, a bright and very able cellular immunologist who had worked with Niels Jerne, joined my laboratory and became my closest collaborator. There was the excitement of ideas that worked, devising and anticipating new experiments, interpreting results, sharing satisfaction or disappointment.

I think I can look back with enough objectivity to recognize patterns of strength as well as a characteristic inadequacy in my own research career. We were always working on important questions, and I often came up with new, improved experimental methods for examining a problem. We contributed to innovative techniques for chemical modification and manipulation of antibody molecules, for purifying antibodies, for affinity labeling of certain enzymes and receptor molecules on cell membranes, for isolating specific cell populations, for enhancing fluorescence visualization of structures on a cell surface, and for using antibodies to target selected cells with toxic agents. This catalogue of our efforts will not convey much to the uninvolved, but quite a few of these advances found wide application in immunological and biochemical research laboratories. Our laboratory sustained a good international reputation.

What I did not achieve was the definitive study of any one significant phenomenon in the make-up and function of the immune system. I did not set my sights on a particular biological mystery and stay with it until it was solved. I am probably not objective enough to explain why. Perhaps I came to biology too late and in too much of a hurry to feel thoroughly prepared and at home. Research was always important to me, but, except for a frenetic period during and after my all too brief (three year) Ph.D. program, it was not the all-consuming interest that drives the best scientists I have known. Perhaps, however, even if I had suppressed the pull of other interests and of turbulent times, I would not have acquired the exceptional scientist's full measure of bold conjecture, insight, and concentrated perseverance.

Be that as it may, there remains substantial pride in what our laboratory did accomplish.

Between 1967 and 1977, I was Chair of the Department of Microbiology and Immunology, initially for a five year term and, after a welcome interval, for another three years. The onerous aspect of heading a department, the administrative load, can be balanced by opportunities to influence the way things are done. The department's input on academic and personnel matters is determined by faculty decisions, but the chairperson's role can be decisive. My agenda highlighted strengthening the graduate program in immunology and establishing affirmative action in personnel appointments and student admissions. In addition to expanding and improving our courses, we were able to bring outstanding immunologists from around the world to teach and work with our students for periods ranging from a week to a semester. Four women joined our department faculty, where there had previously been none. During this time, there were still no women faculty members in the departments academically closest to ours, Biochemistry and Molecular Biology. The most important change was that our graduate program was opened up to African-American and, later, Latino students, eight of whom went on to Ph.D. or M.D. degrees.

I remember the first graduate student of color whom we accepted. He eventually got both his Ph.D. (at Berkeley) and an M.D. (at UC San Francisco). But the going was very rough.

He came from a small Southern black college whose white faculty sent a letter of recommendation that no one had even bothered to check for atrocious grammar and spelling. On the strength of a more instructive letter from Howard University, where he had spent a year after college, our faculty was finally persuaded to admit him. Four years later, when he received his Ph.D., he gave a commencement address that startled the faculty and his fellow students. He told just what it was like to be the first graduate student of color—scrutinized and always doubted, under pressure to prove that his presence was deserved, that he was not an academic welfare recipient. I recalled the comment of a faculty colleague after the student's sterling performance at his Ph.D. Oral Examination: she was relieved he did exceptionally well because she had been afraid she would be expected to "bend over backward" to pass him.

In the early 1980s, two exceptional graduate students, Jeri Hill and Olivia Martinez (now Ph.D.'s), and a post-doctoral fellow, Jerry Guyden (now a biology professor at CCNY), made our department a gathering place for students of color, undergraduates as well as graduates, in all biology departments. Sympathetic faculty were welcome participants. Here, individual difficulties and grievances were discussed, tutoring took place, and representations were made to faculty where insensitivity or prejudice was encountered. We brought to the Chancellor and the police chief the complaint of black students and employees who were repeatedly confronted for proof that they "belonged" on campus, even at gun point when coming back after dark for laboratory tasks. A nationwide recruiting program to attract minority students, initiated earlier in the Zoology Department, took shape.

One year Jeri Hill and I drove together through Alabama and Mississippi to give workshops in Immunology at several black colleges. At Tugaloo College in Mississippi, we had to overcome the refusal of the faculty, none of whom were black, to recognize Jeri, an African-American woman, as the teacher in charge of the cell biology portion of the workshop. We did attract two Tugaloo students to graduate work at Berkeley, where both have since achieved Ph.D. degrees.

The major project of our student-faculty group in 1984 was to organize a two day teach-in on affirmative action for the faculty in all biology departments. Progress has since been made in admissions, but not yet with respect to faculty recruitment.

I retired from teaching in 1984, before my sixty third birthday. My laboratory remained active for another three years. Deciding to become an Emeritus Professor well before the mandatory retirement age of seventy was unusual at that time. It was several years before the budget crunch had induced the Regents to offer the "Golden Hand Shake," a special package of retirement benefits aimed at making it attractive for professors to take early retirement. In fact, I signed my retirement papers shortly after Governor Deukmejian announced that the following two years would bring an 18% pay raise for UC faculty, the first significant increase in a long while. I swallowed once or twice, but signed my papers anyway.

I had planned for a long time to retire early enough to have some years in which I could again put my addiction to the future foremost. So much had changed and was changing still more. What I wanted was not a reprise, not a repeat of old experiences, but unrestricted time to rethink my ideas, to write, to be active on critical issues. For that I wanted freedom from over twenty years of grant deadlines, intensive teaching, and "running" a lab. I enjoyed and valued my academic years fully, but now I felt another need.

Other things also kept me from delaying my retirement decision. Beginning in 1983, Roz had a series of back and hip surgeries that involved stretches of serious disability and that left her, even after recovery, with chronic pain.

Then, too, I saw an ugly side to the coming of age of molecular biology and immunology as fields for booming commercial enterprise and speculation. The culture and practices of the biological research community were changing in some unpleasant ways. In 1982, I gave a talk to a large audience of Berkeley biology faculty and students on the topic, *Biology and the University on the Market Place: What's for Sale?* The rush of faculty and university administrators to capitalize on the promise created by many years of publicly funded research was on. New venture capital enterprises began to mushroom, and giant corporations were also moving in. In the climate of the Reagan era, there would be little concern for social responsibility or public involvement in setting policy and priorities. One could foresee some negative consequences for the university and for biology, and these are today's reality: sponsorship and support from private enterprises are now a necessary measure of success for young professors; conflicts of interest abound and secrecy restricts scientific exchange; more laboratories impose strict rules and tight control over students and fellows; vital research materials are privatized, and the Supreme Court decrees that everything, including research animals and living human tissue, can be patented.

Among the companies that approached our laboratory, one was particularly interested in the fact that we had chemically attached a powerful toxin to antibody molecules. We had adapted a method that was not original with us, but we were the first laboratory to apply it to synthesizing toxin-antibody conjugates in general, and the first to prepare such conjugates with monoclonal antibodies. The hope was that one could eventually come up with "magic bullets" that would be directed by antibody to find and kill targeted cancer cells. We declined to get involved with the company, although we pointed out to its representative that experiments showed that the conjugates did not behave predictably and were far from the desired "magic bullet." The company went ahead without us. To this day, some ten years later, it is still capitalizing on "magic bullet" hype although relevant experimental results in many laboratories are clearly disappointing.

The excitement and accomplishments of research would always outweigh the unpleasant changes of recent years, but I was ready to move on and had no desire to adjust to the new environment.

For more than a year prior to retirement, I had joined with four faculty colleagues from the departments of History and Political Science in a project on Alternatives to the Cold War. The project received support from UC's Institute on Global Conflict and Cooperation and from the California Council for the Humanities. We convened conferences in June 1983 and November 1984, and a book, *Before the Point of No Return,* was published in 1986. The book, which I edited, offered replies from many prominent political analysts to the question: *Do you think peaceful termination of the Cold War is a real possibility in the foreseeable future? If so, under what circumstances?*

Most who answered saw no such possibility in the offing. Some of us, though, argued that the Cold War was becoming an unsustainable burden for *both* sides, even though more for the USSR than for the USA, and that a turn away from the Cold War might indeed be forthcoming.

These were strange years, the 1980s. Public acceptance, with enthusiasm, of Reagan and Thatcher left most liberals and leftists without hope. On the other hand, from 1986 on there were growing indications that the Cold War, and with it the threat of nuclear war, might be receding. The emergence of

Gorbachev and "new thinking" mixed exaggerated international hope with continuing despair over domestic politics.

On campus, there were sporadic, but sometimes impressive movements on social issues. For several years running, there were large actions blockading the Livermore nuclear weapons center which, along with the Los Alamos facility, is linked to the University of California. Massive actions against UC's investments in South African apartheid forced a stubborn Board of Regents and, eventually, the State of California to divest. Both of these movements were met with repeated mass arrests. Together with some of my faculty colleagues, I was arrested for participating in the Livermore blockade and, again, for a sit-in at University Hall by Faculty Against Apartheid.

The most persistent issue-centered organization on campus during the 1980s was Faculty for Human Rights in Central America. This began in 1982 as a response to death squad atrocities in El Salvador, kidnappings and murders, and armed attacks on the University of San Salvador. It later focused on US policy toward Nicaragua, opposing both the Contra War and the economic blockade. It sent numerous faculty delegations to report on human rights and US policy in all countries of Central America. In 1984, I went to Nicaragua to participate in a conference on public health and medical problems.

Since retirement, my involvement in academic affairs has waned by my own choice. I remain interested, however, in the push and pull of efforts to achieve cultural diversity on a campus and in a state in which people of color are becoming the majority. I also take part in cross disciplinary exploration of social issues related to genetic engineering and the biotechnology explosion.

My main preoccupation has been to take in and try to understand the vast, unexpected changes that have erupted as the lid was lowered on the Cold War. I wrote several articles on the great hopes generated by Gorbachev and on the disastrous finale for the former USSR. Then, too, there is the deep crisis in every facet of US society, astonishingly revealed in the wake of the Cold War and so soon after the Gulf War diversion. More than anything else, the shock of these events has spawned this book.

I will mention one more twist in our personal circumstances, Roz's and mine, before closing this short history. On October 20th, 1991, we lost our home in the Oakland-Berkeley fire storm. Like almost all our fellow victims, we got out just ahead of the fire and lost everything we had accumulated. Most of it will not be sorely missed, as insurance allows us to fill the material void with new acquisitions from tooth brushes to furniture, pots and pans to stereo and TV. Some things we can never replace in kind, and will try to hang on to in memory. These are the things that a friend meant when she wept "you lost your history." Only a couple of these items also had significant monetary value, a marvelous Charles White etching that was a gift from his widow and children only a few months before the fire, and a William Gropper drawing given by the artist to my father many years ago. Then there was the correspondence, and the clippings, the reminders of precious moments, of family and comrades, of recognition and awards that came to Carla and David, of shared experiences and struggles. We would even have liked to keep the death threats mailed to us after my encounter with Ronald Reagan in 1969. I know that if we still had my FBI file, I would refer to it from time to time, but I don't think it's worth bothering to try to get it again.

We won't rebuild. This fire was not the first in our neighborhood. Forty homes burned down in 1970, but ours escaped the fire that time. It was saved by a close co-worker from my laboratory at UC, John Kimura, while Roz and I were away on sabbatical leave at the Pasteur Institute in Paris. John's courage gave us a twenty-one year respite until the fire next time. In all, twenty five good years were lived in the only home we ever owned. During that time our children married and shaped their lives in ways that we admire, and our extended family is warm and close. Three grandchildren, now in their teens, remember the old house fondly.

Now, however, home is a rented apartment overlooking Lake Merritt in downtown Oakland. It's time for me to look around, to look at the world over the span of my three score and ten years, to find my own links between past and present—and perhaps a clue or two to some corner of the future.

PART II

RETROSPECTIVE ON THE COMMUNIST JOURNEY

CHAPTER 5

SIDES

Where has the journey I've described taken me so far?

It has changed some of my opinions and added dramatically to the number of questions without answers. Probably it hasn't much altered the values I grew up with, or my attitudes toward my country.

I have worn no defining political label since I left the Communist Party a very long time ago. I look at the future and, for that matter, at the present and the past, with wonder and uncertainty. But there is some ground to stand on while the search continues. I believe it is still worth answering the cutting question in the old union song: "Which side are you on?"

In the culture of the 1992 Presidential election campaign, the expected answer was that everyone should be on the same side—"pro-business, pro-labor, and pro-recovery," as one presidential candidate described himself. Yet, in a society so profoundly divided by criteria of wealth, privilege, and color, there are sides to take. Modern society has created critical problems that result in shared concerns for the vast majority of the population, but survival still has a very different meaning for oppressor and oppressed. So, while much has changed since Karl Marx identified the struggle of oppressed classes as the key to social progress, that principle I accept now as much as in the past.

My respect for the complexity of our society, for what distinguishes our country and its strikingly diverse people, has grown. I am as convinced as ever that inequality and injustice is endemic to the structure of our capitalist society, which dominates the behavior of our government on domestic matters and as a world power. I also know that this is a dynamic country, many of whose accomplishments and values inspire loyalty—even among those who are deprived of most of its benefits. Abroad there is much about the USA that is widely admired, as well as much in its behavior that is feared and bitterly resented.

My own experience with repressive and punitive actions of government has been countered, to my distinct personal advantage, by the commitment of many people to fairness and to the First Amendment. I have every reason to appreciate the potential in the United States for people to intervene, despite a limited and rigged electoral system, to deal with reactionary excesses, to bring to heel the "man on a white horse" who shows up all too often. There are many countries, probably most, where a lifetime of opposition to the powers that be would bring prison, torture, and death. Of course, too many of our own people have met such a fate, some in political persecutions and labor struggles, many more simply because of their color or the conditions in which they live.

The modern history of most nations, certainly ours, is heavily scarred by abominations, atrocities, even genocide. Thinking about the future, though, the thing that seems most suggestive to me is that our history shows the power of people to effect change. Like Marx, Frederick Douglass emphasized the connection between progress and struggle, and our history makes the case. Always too slow, and sometimes much too bloody, that is the way we have moved from the Bill of Rights to the abolition of slavery, to women's suffrage, to unionization, to social security, to wiping out segregationist laws. Nothing that has happened in my lifetime, and nothing I see today, lessens my belief in that process.

I feel a stronger identification than ever with the desire for change that is swelling up again in the country. That desire, and the needs and emotions that cause it, may prove too profound to be simply subsumed as an election year cliché.

For years, socialists and even liberals have had to contend with being labeled Un-American by corrupt demagogues who debased the country with sham patriotism. I don't feel estranged from the majority of people in the way I relate to my country. The mix of emotions and attitudes varies, but experience tells me that most of us who feel lucky to be here have reason to temper pride in country with some anger and shame about how many Americans live. Similarly, if more ambiguously, most of us have felt at least occasional discomfort over our government's role abroad, especially as protector of so many oppressive regimes from Haiti to South Africa, Vietnam to El Salvador.

My own search connects with the mood overtaking so many Americans as we realize where we are at the end of the Twentieth Century. There must be a better way to live, better values, better vibes between people, better things to reach for. For me, that is where aspirations toward socialism are born, even as experience proves that the meaning of socialism has to be discovered anew.

CHAPTER 6

USSR: THE ROAD AFTER OCTOBER

For a large part of my life, I felt that the revolution led by Lenin in October, 1917 was the most promising event of the twentieth century. I was among the many around the world who thought we were living through the greatest epoch of social change in human history. The Russian people had shown it could be done and others would find their own paths to a just society. Humanity was at the threshold of liberation from all forms of exploitation based on class, race, or gender. Our generation would see the downfall of capitalism, a system driven by greed for profits, and the growth of socialism, a system based on principles of economic and social justice.

So much has changed. The USSR is no more. The end of the Cold War brings eleventh hour release from the horrendous nuclear confrontation between superpowers, but there is no relief from the bitter fact of a world still torn by cruel wars and more divided than ever into the rich few and the impoverished many. Humanity is a long way from "free at last."

I do not take the collapse of the Soviet Union as the final judgment on socialism's future, or on the place of the communist movement in the history of this century. It is surely not the vindication of capitalism. The unstable world of misery and inequality that capitalism dominates today is far from gaining acceptance as the last word in human relations and social progress. How could history end here? The search and struggle for a better fate, for something finer in the way human beings live, is as constant as the will of millions of people not to succumb to conditions of slavery and suffering. It is as inevitable for us and for future generations as the diverse reasoning that made Karl Marx and Vladimir Lenin, George Bernard Shaw and Jean Paul Sartre, Albert Einstein and W.E.B. Du Bois advocates of socialism.

All the more reason, then, to ask what went wrong—or, how do I see *now* the things I saw, or thought I saw, *before*? Let me look first at the Union of Soviet Socialist Republics, the seventy-four year phenomenon at the center of the hopes, fears, and storms that shook our twentieth century world.

I was unsuspecting and uncritical before 1956 despite the welter of contrary evidence. I did not distinguish evidence, that should have been convincing to any open mind, from hate propaganda directed against the very idea of a socialist state. How could credence have been rendered to tortured confessions recited at the Moscow Trials to "legalize" the murder of most old Bolsheviks? It is hard to imagine, in retrospect, the mind state that never conceived it possible that Stalin could lie, even when that required believing the unbelievable.

Once blind faith gave way to undeniable truth, there was room for reason to grow. I continued to attach enormous importance to the place of the Soviet Union in the worldwide constellation of struggles to overcome imperialism's harvest of fascism, wars, racism, and colonialism. But the contradictions in Soviet society, the deep and frequent collisions between stated principle and actual behavior, brought recognition that only a fundamental turn—away from reliance on vast military power, on forceful control over Eastern Europe, on censorship and suppression of dissent—could salvage the original promise of a new day in human history.

I was overjoyed when Gorbachev focused on the very things that I believed most fervently: first, that the compelling moment had come for both sides to end the Cold War and the US–Soviet nuclear face-off; and second, that the salvation of Soviet society demanded nothing less than a revolutionary transformation toward democratic socialism. I cried when the last hope for that revolution ended in the chaos of the August 1991 coup and the final collapse of the USSR.

On balance, what did the Soviet Union's seventy-four years mean for the world?

"Balance" is not the right word. For me, the negatives and the positives of Soviet history are both off scale. Soviet achievements don't mitigate the evil, nor do its failures cancel historic contributions.

For anyone with mind and conscience, the cost of the evil is measured most of all in the enormous numbers of lives sacrificed to the power and paranoia of Stalin. The assault on human rights, on truth and on the courage to speak honestly, was massive under Stalin and remained pervasive even after his exterminist methods were condemned and halted upon his death.

The failures were in the model that evolved for achieving socialism, a model based on a command economy driven by the centralized authority of the Communist Party. That top-heavy model worked spectacularly to achieve highly focused and difficult goals, notably the building of heavy industry, military might, and, later on, space research. It grew stagnant as bureaucracy became overwhelming and eventually corrupt, too rigid to cope with the diversity of modern economic problems and unprecedented technological change, unable to encourage initiative and to satisfy consumer needs. Certainly the pressures of the forty year Cold War took their toll on the Soviet economy (and, as we now see, on the US economy as well).

The ultimate failure was in conceiving of socialism without democracy, despite convoluted protestations to the contrary. It was at its worst in the maintenance, by military force, of satellite regimes in Eastern Europe. The ultimate cost was the overwhelming anger that finally swept these regimes away and then finished off the USSR itself.

Still, against that starkly tragic canvas, I must recognize contrasting contributions of great value. Perhaps the influence of Marxist dialectics causes me to acknowledge the coexistence and conflict of opposite impulses inherent in the first great socialist experiment. The movement that hailed Stalin for twenty odd years, and put his clones at the helm of a number of Communist parties, also energized millions of idealistic, selfless, creative, and brave human beings who did more than any other political formation to advance social justice. This was testimony to the inspiration of the socialist vision, but also to the need to respond to the disasters inflicted on humanity by twentieth century capitalism.

In less than three decades, the capitalist system generated two world wars, the most devastating international economic crisis in history, and a global fascist axis that organized genocide and came close to enslaving the world. Through it all, inhumanly oppressive colonial empires were maintained and exploited on every continent. Anyone who thinks the world would have been better off without the Russian Revolution ought to consider where we would be without its impact everywhere on resistance to the old order.

No history of popular struggle for social change since 1917, in any part of the world, can leave out the extraordinary role of men and women inspired by the challenge of the first socialist revolution. Over the years many turned away in disillusionment from the Soviet Union and its leaders, but still took inspiration and ideas from Marx and Lenin, and from individual communists viewed as folk heroes and sages in more than a few national liberation movements. My point is not to give all credit to communists, or to hide unforgivable pages of shame in the ledger. Yet only blatant revisionist history can fail to record the prominent place of communists in the defeat of Hitler and Mussolini, in the shattering of colonial empires after World War II, in expanding trade unions and the rights of workers, in combating racist structures in the United States and South Africa, in organizing the poor and the oppressed against oligarchic military dictatorships, and lots more. 1917 did not usher in world socialism, but it opened a period in which world capitalism became vulnerable to a host of popular struggles. I believe it changed the scope of what is possible, of what social movements can hope to accomplish. More on that later.

The Soviet Union itself pioneered a series of advanced social rights—to free education, literacy, health care, and employment—that workers in other countries later demanded and sometimes won partially through liberal social legislation. These rights were intrinsic to the Soviet social system. Their universal character did not, however, keep Communist Party favoritism from flourishing, or prevent political and ethnic bias and the shame of recurring anti-Semitism.

The supreme achievement of the Soviet people was their crucial role and immense sacrifices in the triumph over Hitler's war machine. After World War II, whatever critique can be made of Soviet priorities and policies, the USSR became the major force to which many Third World countries and independence movements looked for support. For a country to rise so rapidly from the backwardness of Czarism, and from the incredible devastation inflicted by the Nazis, to become so significant a factor in world affairs, is one of the major wonders of this century—no less astonishing, perhaps, than its remarkably sudden disintegration.

My rethinking of the Soviet experience focuses on the actual circumstances that conditioned developments in our century, on the historic context rather than on the abstract rightness or wrongness of theoretical propositions associated with Marxism or Marxism-Leninism. With its creation in 1917, the Soviet Union broke away not only from its backward Czarist past, but from a world system in which all economic, political, and military power was in the hands of the most developed capitalist states.

Lenin recognized a cardinal revolutionary reality that was to produce the basic dilemma of socialist experience in the Twentieth Century. His observation that capitalist society's chain would break at its weakest link proved true not only for the Russian Revolution but for every victorious revolution thereafter. Revolutions erupted where oppression was most intolerable and where rulers were most reactionary and incompetent. The corollary truth was that these revolutions occurred invariably in backward countries that lacked the economic and social foundations for socialist development. Moreover, every breakaway nation confronted a world economy dominated by imperialism and an unyielding hostility punctuated by devastating wars and economic boycotts. Every such country, first of all the Soviet Union itself, faced the need to navigate a difficult and prolonged transition that precluded a direct path to socialist society.

That analysis is shared by many socialists today. I think it needs to be kept in focus in order to evaluate how the dilemma was met in the past and with what consequences for the present. Even more relevant, aspects of the historic problem persist and bear on the critical choices facing socialist movements and governments now in a world very different from that of 1917.

No revolution in history faced more adverse conditions and more devastating assaults than those that came close to destroying the USSR between 1917 and 1945. The question is not whether a developed socialist society could have been achieved in the USSR under the prevailing circumstances. Rather it is to what extent it was possible for the revolution to develop a democratic character and an ever greater base of popular support at home and internationally. To what extent could a besieged revolutionary country rely on its moral and political reserves rather than on an overriding priority of dictatorial force? Could a democratic path provide the flexibility and stability necessary to thwart efforts to crush the revolution or divert it from socialist goals?

The fact is that the history which produced the dilemmas also offered choices. There were forks in the road. Nobody knows where the unchosen roads would have led.

At the outset, there was hope that the fledgling Soviet state would not have to go it alone. The ravages and chaos created by World War I raised the possibility of socialist revolution in the heart of industrial Europe, especially in defeated Germany. That prospect remained, and actually grew as post-war economic crisis deepened, until it was diverted disastrously by the victory of fascist "national socialism" in Italy and then Germany.

Meanwhile, the new Soviet Union was bled by military intervention and starved through economic blockade organized by the victorious allies, led by the United States. It didn't take Lenin long to realize that survival required breaking economic isolation, encouraging the development of a mixed economy through his New Economic Policy (NEP) introduced in the early nineteen twenties. Along with the publicly owned sectors, private capital and initiative had to be accepted in a regulated market economy. Harsh emergency measures, deemed necessary during the interventionist and civil war period that followed the revolution, had to be relaxed in order to improve relations between workers in the cities and peasants on the countryside.

That choice was aborted under Stalin, who opted instead for virtual war on the private sector, especially the peasantry. An horrendous price in lives and liberty was exacted by the campaign to press all of agriculture into large collective farms, which would feed the workers in the rapidly growing state-owned industries. Stalin was determined to build heavy industry by any means necessary. He warned prophetically, in 1931, that the Soviet Union had only ten years to become an advanced industrial nation or be destroyed in the war which actually did come when Hitler's army invaded in 1941. Since prophecy did become fact, the rationale for Stalin's pre-war industrial policy cannot simply be tossed aside. That doesn't say there was no other way, or that the ruthless approach to collectivization was an asset rather than a destructive force. Nor is there any question that the Soviet Union was weakened by Stalin's disastrous military and political purges, and discredited by his desperate dealings around the short-lived Nazi-Soviet Non-Aggression Pact of 1939.

The biggest catastrophe for the Soviet Union was that with Stalin in power, society lost its capacity to choose. More important than the fateful decisions made on economic policy was the ruthless extermination of dissent and dissenters. With that, Soviet society lost not only moral strength, but the potential for self-correction.

I don't agree with interpreters who try to equate Lenin and Stalin. It's not just that Lenin, while ill and close to death, warned against Stalin's abuse of power and urged that he not be entrusted with leadership of the Party. Nor is it because Stalin became madly, terribly paranoid. Lenin's writings, while fiercely polemical, are the work of a major mind. He was the most significant disciple of Marx in this century. He didn't simply parrot Marx, but extended the analysis of capitalism to new features of imperialism and international finance that emerged in the twentieth century. He was an exceptional creature of his times, not an oracle for all times. His views on communist parties and on the exercise of state power were conditioned by a lifetime of revolutionary struggle against the most brutal and autocratic regime in Europe. While Lenin, in his last years, was focusing on new conditions and seeking greater flexibility, Stalin was able to consolidate a highly centralized form of party organization that Lenin himself had promoted.

How the gift of more years would have been used by Lenin is a silly question, seductive though it is. We do know that the greatest abuse of his legacy was Stalin's creation of what he called "Marxism-Leninism," the set of dogmas used to define heresy and to wipe out all opposition. In the name of Lenin, Stalin outlawed altogether the vigorous debate that Lenin and his comrades deemed essential to reaching decisions on policy. He thus closed the door to creativity and change, and began the process of rigor mortis that eventually offset the impressive social gains of the revolution.

After the end of World War II, there were democratic alternatives that might have enhanced the appeal and possibilities of progress toward socialism. True, the Soviet Union was devastated by the war and the United States emerged as the strongest power of all time. The return by Truman and

Churchill to the old anti-Soviet and anti-socialist formulas was unmistakable even before the end of the war, a message conveyed to the USSR in the mushroom clouds over Hiroshima and Nagasaki. That was the beginning of an extended US policy mission that, for the duration of the Cold War, asserted its power in support of every declared anti-communist regime no matter how tyrannical and corrupt. Nevertheless, the prestige of the Soviet Union in 1945 was immense, socialism was experiencing a level of popular international support hitherto unmatched, and anti-colonialism was sweeping the world. These were great sources of strength on which to build a lasting socialist presence in the world community, to boldly pursue peaceful coexistence and competition, and to thwart strategies aimed at a new anti-Soviet military crusade.

What choices did the USSR have when confronted by the US government's determination to stem the post-war anti-imperialist tide and to make this the "American Century?" After Truman introduced the world to atomic horror, no rational argument could be made against Soviet refusal to accept a US monopoly on atomic and nuclear weaponry. Nor could the USSR decline to exert its influence in support of struggles for self-determination in the Third World. Nevertheless, basic questions persist about priorities, choices, and their consequences in the development of Soviet society and policy during the Cold War era. In general, the risks of democratic development were shunned in favor of matching the US at any cost in the superpower arms race. With Stalin still alive, the answer to the Cold War challenge was to seal off Eastern Europe completely and take no chances on political processes that might conceivably resurrect hostile regimes on the borders of the USSR. The Soviet Union itself was again cordoned off from effective cultural interaction with the rest of the world. Although the worst features of Stalinist practice were soon vigorously renounced during Khrushchev's tenure, that first promising break with the past was aborted and not permitted to grow into a commitment to democratic socialist development.

Probably the most crucial fork in the road came with the Czechoslovak Spring of 1968. Why was 1968 not the turning point? Why was the answer tanks rather than an opening to democratic socialism? Why the Brezhnev Doctrine rather than an historic initiative to break down the Cold War, as took place under far more difficult circumstances in 1989. In 1968, there was popular enthusiasm in Eastern Europe for "socialism with a human face," and opposition in the US to the Vietnam War was becoming a huge problem for the Cold Warriors and the Pentagon. It is hard to avoid the conclusion that the choice at that time was more a matter of the CPSU's conservatism— fear of democracy and a lack of confidence in the people— rather than a heightened military threat to the Soviet Union from the West.

By subordinating political and moral considerations to traditional military logic, the USSR actually became more vulnerable to the pressures of the Cold War. It was made inevitable that Eastern Europe would one day erupt in a popular tide of rebellion. Refusing to risk democratic alternatives meant the further build-up of stagnation and rigidity in Soviet society. It contributed also to increasing Soviet isolation from international scientific and cultural exchange, a state of affairs eagerly fostered by US Cold War strategy. While focusing on military and space technology, the Soviet Union remained largely insulated from the scientific and technological revolutions that in recent years have altered the world economy and given capitalism renewed advantage.

One may speculate about how much the balance of nuclear terror contributed to preventing the Cold War from turning hot. The decision not to use atomic weapons in Korea and in Vietnam was probably based less on military calculation than on projections of disastrous political consequences for the government that would reinitiate the calamity of nuclear warfare. Prevention of World War III has not resulted primarily from the way both sides played the deadly game of military chess. The overwhelming factor has been *political*, the realization that the nuclear age brings humanity face to face with the prospect of its own extinction.

When Gorbachev succeeded the last of a line of octogenarians as head of the Party and of the State, in 1986, a choice was finally made for a different course. At that stage, it proved easier to leave the old road than to chart a new one.

CHAPTER 7

USSR: LOST LAST CHANCE

When Gorbachev moved so irresistibly to force an end to the Cold War, when he launched *glasnost* and *perestroika*, my hopes for the world were higher than at any time since the final defeat of the fascist Axis in 1945.

Was this illusion again?

As things worked out, I suppose that has to be conceded. But, as I try to persuade myself and will argue later, we are at a place in history where a better world may not be an impossible dream. I did recognize, from the beginning, that the Soviet Union was in serious trouble, and that the "Gorbachev revolution" might not be able to overcome. That didn't keep me from cheering it on until Gorbachev himself began to give up on it, finally surrendering in almost total isolation from his own people.

When Marxists try to analyze a major political development, there is a lot of weighing of "objective and subjective factors." If there is a setback, how much was due to unavoidable circumstance (objective conditions) and how much to human error (miscalculation and mistakes)? Both were present aplenty during the last years of the USSR.

In 1986, conditions were ripe for ending the forty year Cold War, and Gorbachev was the first head of state to act on the basis of that awareness. While the Soviet Union was hurting the most, the burdens of an insane arms race were putting the United States at a disadvantage in its growing economic rivalry with Japan and Germany. It, too, needed to adjust to a rapidly changing global economy. Prospects were poor for military solutions to the many proxy wars that punctuated the Cold War. Just as the Soviets were experiencing in Afghanistan, US engagement in large scale military intervention had suffered stalemate in Korea and humiliating failure in Vietnam. The people in countries decimated by military intervention were desperately weary of seemingly endless civil warfare. Above all, people everywhere were weary of a world paralyzed by the Cold War, where burgeoning problems of human survival were kept off the agenda, held hostage to the superpower confrontation.

So, in breaking with the Cold War, Gorbachev's leadership was in solid harmony with objective necessity.

There is no doubt, also, that internal and external problems had brought the USSR, and all countries in its sphere, to a depth of crisis that could no longer be covered over. I believe Gorbachev was right in declaring that Soviet renewal required a revolutionary departure from old ways, toward honesty and openness (*glasnost*), toward economic restructuring (*perestroika*), toward a socialism that could only be achieved on the basis of democracy. From that point on, however, I find it hard to reach conclusions about the extent to which the mounting obstacles and dismal outcome were dictated by accumulated harsh realities, as opposed to flaws in judgment and policy.

Why do I see the outcome as dismal when it is hailed by statesmen of the West as an unprecedented triumph for democracy and capitalism?

I believe that the reforms initiated by Gorbachev advanced democracy in a major way, but I don't believe that all of the factors and machinations that tore the Union apart can be attributed to democracy. Democratic development was far from sufficient to allow full popular participation and deliberate choices about how and where to proceed. Moreover, our media's repetition in one breath of "democracy and capitalism" fails to make either the necessary byproduct of the other. Capitalism has proven capable of accommodating to the most tyrannical dictatorships and worst violations of human rights all over the world.

Dismal, to say the least, is the eruption of nationalist and ethnic antagonisms and warfare in the former Soviet Union and Eastern Europe. Neither that part of the world, nor the world as a whole, is better off with the political and cultural fragmentation, economic disarray, and subservience to the International Monetary Fund that breeds growing disillusionment and anger in place of once high hopes.

Some of Gorbachev's critics, in China for example, maintain he should not have begun by proclaiming *glasnost,* since it invited a torrent of attacks on the system and opened the door to chaos. Rather he should have begun a gradual program of economic renewal, introducing some market reforms while preventing major disruption of the existing fabric of Soviet society. Of course, China still has to prove its own formula: can a strongly authoritarian regime evolve into a socialist democracy by tightly controlling the timing and degrees of freedom to be allowed? At what point do they allow multiple forms of political expression and organization? When do they risk relaxing control? When do they take a chance on the unpredictability of democratic elections?

Whatever difficulties resulted from the historically belated turn toward democracy in the Soviet Union, I think that only a bold move in that direction offered hope for substantial change. The economy had become incredibly rigid and cumbersome, encrusted with top-down bureaucracy and unable to respond to elementary consumer needs. The expectation of Gorbachev and the comrades who initially surrounded him was that *glasnost* would generate popular enthusiasm and infuse society with a new spirit of participation and initiative that would propel *perestroika* forward. That never came about.

They expected that the Communist Party would transform itself and set the pace for the new revolution. Instead, the Party that defined itself as the "vanguard" fell badly behind. As the main locus of entrenched bureaucracy and privilege, it incurred the wrath of millions—not just for past sins, but because much of the party apparatus stubbornly resisted each advance toward democratic political and economic reform.

Still, they were unprepared for what would come when a highly controlled society found itself unfettered. *Glasnost* vented all the pent-up bitterness, all the suppressed ethnic identities and long-nurtured internecine hatreds, all the cynicism over lies and doublespeak, all the hidden traditions, fundamentalist religious beliefs, ancient prejudices and superstitions.

The extent of the hostility and disaffection among the Soviet people came to me as a shock. I did not expect the USSR to go the way of the countries of Eastern Europe. After all, those regimes were headed mainly by old guard Communist Party leaders who were dependent on the Soviet Union's power and were deeply resented. They were also vulnerable to the allure of the relatively prosperous and freer life in neighboring capitalist countries. What was happening in the Soviet Union itself, however, did surprise me, very much.

At various stages in its history, the pride of the majority of its citizens in the achievements of the Soviet Union was unmistakable. Morale had been high in the face of enormous difficulties, especially, but not only, in the anti-Hitler war. Even now, there is manifest attachment to important social and economic rights associated with socialism. Although most social services have been of poor quality and bureaucracy ridden, people expect society to provide free education, health and child care, and job protection. Yet, instead of imbuing people with new motivation to overcome the demoralization left after Brezhnev, Gorbachev, in the end, left a probable majority of his countrymen feeling that socialism itself was either irrelevant or to blame for their sorry condition. And the whirlwinds of nationalism and independence swept away the sense of Soviet or Union identity.

I took Gorbachev's commitment to democratic socialism seriously. I think he viewed democracy and economic reform as essential foundations for a new approach to socialism in the USSR. However, in the year or so prior to the August 1991 coup, saving the Union from imminent dismemberment took precedence for Gorbachev over socialist goals or any other matter of ideology. Given the circumstances, it could hardly have been otherwise.

To understand the eventual failure, I try to picture a hypothetical alternative outcome. What would have constituted success for the socialist project?

It would certainly not have been anything like utopia. It would have been a Union reconstructed on the basis of mutual respect and cooperation among the Republics that chose to remain associated. The primary imperative would have been to make convincing economic headway, involving the people in a process of change by which they could gradually improve their daily lives. This would have meant progress in dismantling bureaucratic Party command over the economy, legitimizing the role of the market, encouraging a mixed economy, and establishing equitable conditions for increasing integration into the global economy. A tall order! But much more was necessary.

If the forces released by this process, especially the emergence of private enterprise, were not to overwhelm the socialist objective, the majority of the people would have to guarantee a government committed to democratic socialist values: one that would promote the public sector and favor society over private interests rather than one loyal to capitalism, domestic and international.

Gorbachev was berated, and his personal downfall blamed, on his prolonged effort to bring the Party along. And, in fact, it was the August coup by the Party hierarchy that gave the final death blow to the Soviet Union and to fading hopes of a "socialist choice." What triggered the coup, however, was Gorbachev's presentation in July of a new Draft Program that was expected to be adopted at a scheduled Communist Party Congress representing its twelve million remaining members. That Program would have changed the Party drastically. Among other things, it accepted the idea of multi-party elections, even though developments pointed to the likelihood that the next President of the Soviet Union would not be a Communist. Without the coup, supporters of democratic socialism both inside and outside the Communist Party might have organized to become an effective influence on the course of the Union. Once again, and for the last time, a conspiratorial Party elite chose the old way with devastating consequences.

What happened to the USSR since 1986 also has to be viewed in a global setting. Gorbachev counted heavily on new post-Cold War relations with the West as a support system for the difficult transformation within the USSR. The worse things got, the more desperately he looked to the United States and Germany.

Gorbachev's heralded "new thinking" did accomplish a remarkable change in world opinion and mood. He brought forward, as no other major political figure had, the urgent problems of global survival. He also, I believe, downplayed some important realities and problems of the post-Cold War world. These, too, contributed to his failures at home. He counted on acceptance of the new Soviet Union as an equal among the leading world powers, but the Bush Administration was tempted to view Soviet misfortune as the opening to "another American Century." Gorbachev's personal popularity in the West soon lost its value among his own people, who reaped no benefit as their own circumstances deteriorated catastrophically.

While Western statesmen had good reason to welcome the reduction in Cold War tensions and nuclear confrontation, they (the US government in particular) were not especially interested in the Soviet Union remaining a great world power. They certainly were not committed to Gorbachev's ideas of saving socialism in a democratic USSR. Bush praised Gorbachev, but withheld any significant economic assistance, even declining to modify Cold War restrictions against the struggling Soviet Union. An influential wing of conservatism within and outside the Administration insisted that we should let Gorbachev go down, since he was trying to rescue socialism—instead we should throw full support to Yeltsin, since he was committed to capitalism and the West. The chief manifesto proclaiming that position was a highly publicized article by "Z," who turned out to be Professor Martin Malia of the UC Berkeley History Department. (Over the years, Malia and I had many debating encounters on the floor of our Academic Senate, as he damned everything about the Free

Speech Movement and opposed all campus activity against the Vietnam War.)

In the end, the great disparity in economic strength between the Soviet Union and the major capitalist powers was decisive in undermining the popular resolve and patience that would have been required for socialist reform. As the USSR was descending into crisis, capitalism in many parts of the world was experiencing a new surge of energy based on a period of striking technological innovations and economic internationalization. On the surface, world capitalism looked healthier at the end of the Eighties than it had in a long time—rosier than it looks now a short while later even in the United States. Of course, the reality of misery in vast areas of the world where capitalism holds sway was always there. That condition seems the likely reward for most of the people in the countries of Eastern Europe.

The hope of help from the G7 powers, particularly the United States, led Gorbachev to a posture of virtual acquiescence to Bush's version of a "new world order." This was an unacknowledged, but significant, departure from Gorbachev's earlier "new thinking" that projected a multi-polar world moving urgently toward equity and justice for underdeveloped nations.

My hope had been that a renewed and democratic USSR, while breaking with Cold War confrontation, would find common cause with the "have not" nations of the world. That might have changed the United Nations and given new spunk to countries held hostage by the IMF. The illusion began to fade in the swift rise of self-centered nationalisms and Russian chauvinism that fostered contempt for the Third World. I remember my dismay when I read article after article in *International Affairs,* the journal of the Soviet Foreign Ministry. The existence of imperialism and neocolonialism was denied, treated as an invention of old line Soviet propaganda; under-developed countries were responsible for their own sorry plight. Even in regard to South Africa, the tilt was to the de Klerk reforms and condescending lectures were directed at the African National Congress. At first I thought these might be individual views, not those of Foreign Minister Eduard Shevardnadze. But events proved otherwise. When Bush commandeered the United Nations for his Gulf War, and blocked any alternative UN strategy to stop Saddam Hussein, Shevardnadze enthusiastically gave the go ahead sign.

The era begun with the Revolution of October, 1917 is over. The effort to renew and extend it by advancing to democratic socialism was itself overwhelmed. In the end, the real life tragedy of the Soviet Union's final five years was like the closing scene of *La Traviata:* a last vibrant aria before the soprano expires. But the soprano comes to life in succeeding operas, in other settings, places, and times.

CHAPTER 8

COMMUNISTS OF THE USA

At the end of 1990, more than thirty-four years after I left the Communist Party, I was invited by the *People's Weekly World*, to contribute one of a series of solicited replies to the question: "Socialism: Can It Happen Here?"

I was surprised by the invitation. The Party editors of the journal had not previously expressed interest in my opinions. I was more surprised at the question. It seemed a peculiar moment, with all that was happening in the world, to focus on socialism in the USA.

My reply was published, for which the editors were berated harshly by the Party's long-time chief, Gus Hall. At a CP National Committee Meeting in January, 1991, Hall presented as a direct quote from my article something he fashioned by condensing, altering, and deleting phrases and sentences— without even dots to indicate omissions. He introduced the "quote" by labeling me as "someone who gave up the struggle 40 years ago." Then he pronounced his verdict: "This is an opportunistic attempt to justify his betrayal 40 years ago. McCarthyism was a tough period. But most Communists stood their ground and fought back." (Hall's "40 years" falsely dated my departure from the Party as 1951 instead of 1956, a convenience necessary to his slander about "betrayal" during the McCarthy period.)

The *People's Weekly World* article reflected my reaction to the crisis of the Communist movement, which in many countries seems to be terminal. Here is part of what I wrote:

SOCIALISM—CAN IT HAPPEN HERE?

The Communists of my youth, myself included, would have had no problem with that question. We knew how to define socialism. We understood the unfolding history that would bring it about. Struggle was indispensable, but we did not doubt that our generation would celebrate the triumph over capitalism.

To ask and answer the question in the same way today, one needs Don Quixote's immunity to reality.

The point is not that the world has gone to pot. On the contrary, there is release from the hellish dead-end of Cold War. While support for socialism has been battered badly, socialists now have a sounder basis for hope and work. But most socialists of every tendency recognize that many former constructs and illusions are finished. Socialism's supporters are not simply going through a temporary adjustment to painful developments, while we wait for experience to reaffirm old "truths." We live in a far different world than we imagined. This surely holds for some conceptions of socialism, and how it would come to pass, that have been basic to communist thought and action.

Current history has dealt drastically with the idea that world socialism would triumph through the agency of vanguard communist parties or the superior example of societies where communists have held power until recently. The communist legacy is mixed, and the mixture is one of extremes. It includes the most heroic and idealistic, and some of the most ignoble, attributes of humanity in the twentieth century. Even where socialist achievements were impressive, efforts to make history conform to dogma—and to force its pace by undemocratic and brutal means—eventually produced deep crisis and mass disillusionment. Communist parties are now severely weakened, divided, or undergoing transformation. In most countries, certainly the United States, they cannot expect mass acceptance as the vanguard of the working class and of the oppressed.

A socialist world will not come about through a relatively short revolutionary epoch. That is not something that can be blamed on, or fundamentally altered by, any theory or political strategy. It is an objective lesson of history.

But while concepts of a sudden revolutionary end to world capitalism are fantasy, both the necessity and the potential for changing the world *in contemporary times* are very real. And this unexpected world can neither be understood nor constructively changed without the contribution of socialist thinking and movements...

With the end of the Cold War, we are entering an era that no one can as yet define with assurance. The compelling necessities of this new era are widely recognized, the unprecedented threat to human survival from nuclear and high-tech war, environmental catastrophe, chronic inequality, massive poverty and racial oppression. But is it realistic to expect significant advances for humanity in a world where capitalism is not about to depart the scene? Socialists will be relevant only if they can answer "yes" and show why and how.

Capitalist societies are not immutable in the face of enormous pressures building in modern society. No government, regardless of social system, can insulate itself from universal concerns involving the fate of this interdependent and endangered world. It is possible to demand and win historic changes toward eliminating war and stopping environmental destruction. It is not unthinkable that we can advance toward a world community that favors greater political and economic equality, focuses on human needs and presents serious roadblocks to racist, oppressive regimes...

Although universal concerns create a qualitatively new outlook, none of the above can happen unless there is also something new in the realm of popular struggle. That, I believe, is to be found in the worldwide rise of a varied array of social and working people's movements that, in common, emphasize democracy and people power. These movements won't transform society in one fell swoop, but they generate socially responsible and socialist answers to problems society cannot push off to a vague and distant future...

Virtually nothing but the name is left today of the Communist Party of the United States. A handful of Gus Hall loyalists cling to a legacy of rigid sectarianism, one that the Party itself tried to shed during its years of significant influence on left and labor politics. After many uninterrupted years of crisis and dwindling membership, a formal "split" occurred in 1992. Those who left the Party, probably a majority, formed The Committees of Correspondence, a temporary organization seeking to stimulate dialogue and cooperative activities among socialists and other leftists.

During my lifetime, no socialist organization had as great an influence as the CPUSA on labor, left-wing movements, and even the general body politic. That has to be put into the perspective of a long-lasting discussion among social and labor historians about "American exceptionalism." Unlike in most capitalist countries, neither a mass socialist organization nor a political party of labor ever took hold in the United States.

There is little question that understanding the role of the United States—past, present and future—is critical to understanding the experience, fortunes, and prospects of socialism not only on home ground, but around the world. Only the USSR has had a greater impact on international socialism. Most analysis of US communist experience, and much concerning the fate of other US left and socialist movements since 1917, has focused on direct and indirect effects of Soviet influence. I would argue, however, that evaluating the US left, including the legacy of US communism, requires primary focus on US society and the changing role of the United States in a changing world.

When I reflect on the fortunes of the CPUSA, I think of two distinct periods. The first begins with the Great Depression and extends through the end of World War II. This is the period in which the crises of US capitalism and the consequences of world imperialism emerged with even more devastating effect than in the years climaxed by the First World War. Fascism and the struggle against it became the defining issue in world and domestic politics. This was the time when, despite numerous ups and downs, the CPUSA grew in influence and played a very significant, often decisive role, on the left.

The second period begins with the emergence from World War II of the USA as *the* capitalist superpower, and covers forty years of Cold War. As the Cold War developed, communist political and ideological influence declined rapidly, especially in the labor movement. The CPUSA lost ability to call the tune on the shape of the left and its strategies. The Party's input was not a major influence on the course of the civil rights movement of the 1950s and '60s, the rise of the New

Left, mass opposition to the Vietnam War, and, more recently, the Jackson presidential campaigns and the Rainbow Coalition, as well as the feminist, pro-choice and environmental movements. This is not to deny the committed participation in these movements of communists and, even more, former communists.

My focus on two periods is meant to indicate a bias, namely, that changes in the historical context have been more important than internal policy choices in affecting the fortunes of socialist movements and the left in the United States. Through decades of warfare over principles and dogma, whether internecine between sects or factional within a given party, the biggest deficits have been inaccurate analysis of the times and how "they are a changing."

The Communist Party was formed in the United States in 1919-1921 (pre-history for the purpose of these reflections from my personal experience). Like all affiliates of the Communist International, its character as a revolutionary vanguard was predicated on an analysis that foresaw imminent socialist revolutions throughout the capitalist world. History did not conform to expectations in any of the developed imperialist countries, but no other socialist organization (including split-offs from the CP) was as prepared for and suited to the storms of the 1930s. Advantages included the very characteristics that eventually became crippling burdens: the Party's commitment to disciplined organization under central control, and its enthusiastic support for the Soviet Union's pioneering effort to build socialism.

Many autobiographical books by disaffected former leaders over the last 25-30 years are strikingly similar in acknowledging major successes for the Party in the 1930s and '40s. While its size and its recognized place in political life never approached what was achieved by fraternal parties in some

Western countries, it became the largest socialist organization and a dynamic influence in many historic left and labor struggles. Joseph Starobin's book, *American Communism in Crisis*, offers the most specific documentation of the Party's organizational gains and expanding influence over almost two decades. The communists gained ground in the course of some major changes of political line, and despite damage inflicted by notoriously abrupt changes of position that corresponded to shifts in Soviet policy.

Why was the CP more significant during this period than any other socialist grouping?

While the initial premise of impending revolution in Western capitalist countries proved wrong, more realistic was communist analysis of imperialism and the capitalist economic crisis, the rise of fascism and the developments that led to World War II. Since the Bolshevik Revolution, anti-communism and anti-Sovietism have been a bigger factor in the United States than in any other capitalist democracy, but that diversion was not enough to keep capitalism's huge problems from dominating the economic and political scene through the '30s and '40s. No other socialist or left organization committed itself as vigorously as the CP to the struggles of the unemployed, to organizing the unorganized and building industrial unions. The CP was first to recognize the historic importance in the United States of "the Negro question" and the struggle against racism. It benefited from and contributed creatively to the "people's front" policies against war and fascism elaborated at the Seventh Congress of the Communist International in 1935. The CP's conditional support for Roosevelt and the New Deal, its emphasis on anti-fascism, and, later, its support for the anti-Axis war set it at loggerheads with Trotskyist, pacifist, and other socialist tendencies. At the same time, it was hurt badly, especially in its influence among intellectuals, by its defense of the Moscow Trials and, most of all, its unquestioning support of the Hitler-Stalin pact.

Without sorting out old and bitter controversies over CP policies, no other socialist grouping was, on balance, as tuned to the struggles and issues of the times from the early '30s through the end of World War II.

Could the CPUSA have become a mass socialist party? How big a role did its mistakes play in the failure of labor and the left to establish a significant political organization?

Most memoirs by those who left the Party in the '50s and '60s pay a great deal of attention to the drastically conflicting views near the end of the Second World War of the two most prominent CP leaders, Earl Browder and William Z. Foster. During the war, Browder, as its operative head, moved to further "Americanize" the Party. The CP was renamed "the Communist Political Association." This was a two-sided statement: it was a drastic departure from original conceptions of the Party dating back to the now dissolved Communist International; it also signaled that the communists did not strive to be a "party" in the sense traditionally defined by the US electoral system. Foster remained a fundamentalist, but his opposition was known only within inner circles at the very top of the leadership. Then, as the earliest signs of breakup of the US-Soviet wartime alliance began to appear, an internationally authoritative French Communist, Jacques Duclos, waded in with an open letter blasting Browder as a "revisionist." The heavy hand of "criticism from abroad" brought about one of those instant changes so characteristic of the Party and so unpalatable to others: overnight "Browderism" became anathema and Foster was crowned.

From the present vantage point in time, events have made a strong case that a Leninist-type vanguard party could not remain viable indefinitely almost anywhere, certainly not in the United States. More interesting retrospectively, however, were the diametrically opposing views on the period that would follow the war. Browder's vision of a long period of peaceful cooperation between capitalist and socialist states was, as he emphasized, a departure from previous Marxist analysis. Foster saw the twin strategic aims of US capitalism as an anti-Soviet world war and domestic fascism, and also insisted that US and world capitalism were on the verge of another great economic crash. On the surface, Foster would seem to have been somewhat closer to reality. But what stands out is that neither provided a sound insight into the nature of the ensuing forty years of Cold War and its consequences within the United States.

Anti-communism indeed became the dominant current in domestic politics and culture once the US government embarked on its new global mission: to revive and take command of the post-war capitalist world, to oppose the spread of socialism and anti-colonial revolutions, and to confront the USSR with an all-out nuclear military build-up. Even in hindsight, one cannot conjure up the resources or a strategy that would have enabled the CPUSA to hold its own through the storms that befell it. Nor were matters helped, as the Cold War began to take shape, by evidence that Stalin had not shed old ways either within the USSR or, especially, in the Soviet control of Eastern Europe.

Nevertheless, a grossly oversimplified analysis that saw fascism as imminent, with world war and depression looming, made for a kind of desperation that hastened the Party's isolation in the labor movement and infected left politics. As the anti-Red and anti-labor offensive swept the country, it was certainly difficult to maintain reasoned equilibrium, to keep in mind critical differences between the situations of post-World War II United States and pre-World War II Germany—differences in history and political traditions, in economic conditions, as well as in the dynamics of world politics.

The system of capitalist democracy in the United States provided the Truman administration with considerable "liberal" maneuvering room on issues, most notably civil rights, which it used effectively in 1948 (along with red-baiting) to dismiss the challenge from the left and a rising peace movement. Analysis, albeit in retrospect, has also to take into account the complexities of a democracy where a vicious Joe McCarthy could dominate the scene in the early 1950s, and "McCarthyism" would become a term of national opprobrium in 1954. The Communist Party resigned itself to an underground mode after the Supreme Court upheld the Smith Act verdicts against its leaders in 1951. It did not (perhaps could not) foresee possibilities that several years later would lead the Supreme Court to overturn the Smith Act, the McCarran Act, and an array of state "loyalty oaths."

Resistance to McCarthyism was not without its shining moments of courage and sacrifice. Nevertheless, by the middle '50s when the underground period ended and major leaders came out of prison, the Party was isolated and weakened beyond any realistic hope for recovery. From that standpoint, the debate that exploded within the CPUSA in 1956, after Khrushchev's 20th Congress revelations on Stalin became known, was an anti-climax.

The debate destroyed the holy fiction of "party unity," opening up fundamental differences over the Party's history and program, its attitude toward Soviet socialism, its very existence. No scenario one might fashion even in hindsight could have restored in 1956 the vitality of the CPUSA as the vehicle through which a significant socialist movement could be built. Certainly, no such possibility was opened up by the party purists, who held on against all internal challenges to their old order even to the present day, decades after the Party ceased to count as an important influence. Any hope for a reasonably effective socialist formation would have required, as a first step, the recognition that neither the CPUSA nor any other existing organization could itself fill the bill.

The notion of a disciplined, self-proclaimed vanguard party was now an illusion and an impediment. For one thing, many people who considered themselves Marxists, especially those in the labor movement, had been compelled to move away from the Party by repressive anti-Communist measures in unions, in schools and universities, and in professions. Did their absence from the Party unmake them as Marxists? Thousands more had been disaffected by Party policies and methods and by its history of absolute hostility to any questioning of the Soviet Union. Were they beyond the pale? Who was to decide what is and is not "true" Marxism?

To make any serious contribution to new forms of cooperation among socialists, the Party would have had to change some of its most basic tenets: its conception of itself as the chosen Marxist-Leninist vanguard, its hostility to other Marxists and to pluralism in socialist ideas, and its ready approval of all aspects of Soviet society and policies. This, of course, would only have been a beginning. Any renewal and eventual regrouping of socialists would have had to depend as well on the readiness of others to depart from their own patterns of sectarianism and futility. Even at that, the combined following of avowedly socialist groupings was far from adequate to the launching of a significant socialist movement.

The CPUSA was not the only or most significant casualty of this second and last period of its history. The unique position of the United States as the superpower of Cold War anti-communism, and as the preeminent capitalist power over a span of fifty years, gave domestic reaction a huge political, economic, social, and cultural boost, culminating in the Reagan-Bush era. This was bad soil for the labor movement, withering numerically and pushed into retreat while enormous shifts were occurring in technology, in industry, and in internationalization of the economy. Powerful social movements appeared at various stages despite, and because of, the arrogance of reaction. However, in the political and cultural atmosphere of Reaganism—and before its economic consequences became manifest to the majority of Americans—the rise of a unified and influential political left was not in the cards.

Another period is just appearing. Internationally, it begins with the end of the US–USSR Cold War confrontation, the collapse of numerous communist regimes, and huge questions about the shape of the post-Cold War world and the future of socialism. Can the United States expect acquiescence to its exclusive superpower role? Can there be international cooperation on the whole range of issues that imperil humanity, or is "new thinking" an illusion? How sharply and in what form will the problems of US capitalism come into focus? As this scene opens, there is no significantly effective socialist organization in the United States. There is no common opinion on what the left is, let alone what it should be. The apparent nadir of the socialist movement may not, however, be the harbinger of what is to come.

In July, 1992, at the founding conference of Committees of Correspondence, I ventured some thoughts on outlook with others who share socialist traditions and vision and who want to contribute to renewed movement on the left:

THE COLLAPSE OF THE USSR: IMPLICATIONS FOR THE LEFT AND FOR THE CAUSE OF SOCIALISM IN A CHANGING WORLD

Talk presented at the founding conference of The Committees of Correspondence, Berkeley, California, July, 1992

Some long-standing strategic conceptions of how socialism would be achieved fell apart with the collapse of the USSR. That is fundamental to the present crisis of socialism. Just as basic is the fact that an alternative strategic outlook for changing the world has yet to come into focus.

For decades, most of us were convinced that we were living at the threshold of the greatest change in human history, the ultimate triumph of socialism over dying capitalism. The camp of socialism and national liberation was growing and would in the foreseeable future demonstrate its superiority. The USSR itself was a powerful force in the worldwide struggle against imperialism, and formerly colonial nations with a large share of the world's population were breaking free of bondage. Of course, some of us were very critical of features of Soviet society and of the interventionist control over Eastern Europe. Nevertheless, we wished or believed that, sooner or later, basic democratic reforms would of necessity take place in the USSR and in the other countries of "actually existing socialism."

But the negative aspects of Soviet society, and of the regimes in its orbit, proved fatal. Correction was too late and too erratic to win the necessary popular support and participation. Instead massive disillusionment, cynicism, disruption and ethnic conflict spelled the end of seventy four years of Soviet rule.

Analysis of what went wrong is far from over. Whether or not the outcome could have been different, what alternatives might have developed in time to set things right, we have to reckon with the consequences of what really did happen. There is no second chance to refurbish and repeat in a better way the historic social experiment that began in 1917.

I don't mean that the struggle for socialism is now less important, or that the contributions of Marxism have lost their value. More than ever, the need is for socialist solutions to problems that, if left to the capitalists, will bury humanity. But a new socialist movement also needs new thinking in a world very different from the one we expected.

Despite important contributions, the "new thinking" that Gorbachev highlighted lost some credibility. His role and message were diminished by catering to US and G 7 priorities as he desperately sought to avert disintegration of the USSR. The value of any new thinking will be canceled out if it denies that progress on the enormous problems of our age requires the struggles of all who are oppressed to change the prevailing world order.

Nevertheless, I think it would be a big mistake to think that the world is back to where it was in 1917. That analogy occurs to some people because of the terrible revival of murderous ethnic wars in Eastern Europe, mainly along fault lines left by imperialism's first world war. Certainly inequality between "haves" and "have-nots," both within and among nations, is greater than it ever was. So is the toll in human life taken by poverty, racism and oppression. But the problems, the conditions for struggle, and the avenues for transforming society are different—in some respects, fundamentally so.

Most of the differences that characterize today's world generate both negative and positive potential.

In the last half century, there has developed a direct and multi-sided threat to humanity's existence. It is valid and necessary to recognize that this unprecedented peril creates universal concerns, even if all elements of society don't have the same values.

The world is interconnected and interdependent as never before. The destructive side of this is that the world economy is dominated by multinational corporations and governed by an imperialist directorate through the IMF. But the growing sense of mutual connection can favor movements for economic and social justice, making the will of the people a powerful international force.

The historic working class and liberation struggles since 1917, in which the Communist experience was by far the most influential, have changed the scope of what is possible in this world. They didn't bring world socialism, but they showed that capitalism is vulnerable, they defeated world fascism, they shattered old colonial empires, they forced important retreats in racist structures, won significant social adjustments in advanced industrial countries, and moved the world away from the edge of nuclear cataclysm.

Capitalism will not disappear in the lifetime of anyone in this room. But its chronic inability to solve the problems that need to be solved now and in the next few lifetimes can undermine its monopoly on power, its capacity to control the fate of nations and of the planet. I wouldn't try to predict the course of struggles for fundamental social change even if I had ten times my allotted seven minutes, but one can foresee the emergence and growth of mixed economies, the possibility of forms of democracy and "people power" that resist manipulation and bribery, and the development of regional and international institutions that take on universal concerns without capitulating to imperialist pressure.

Is it a contradiction to say that progress is possible on every major problem, that society can be significantly transformed—and, simultaneously, that we don't yet foresee the demise of capitalism? Certainly that raises for Marxists, for all socialists, basic questions of theory and practice. I want to pose just one such question. Can democratic forms of state power be achieved that effectively subordinate capitalist interests to those of working people and of society as a whole? We may soon see some answers as a liberated South Africa, and some other countries as well, cope with the development of mixed economies in a democratic political setting.

The biggest questions will arise in developed countries, especially the USA. Only with serious changes here will imperialism's economic stranglehold be released on any and all countries that seek to break historic patterns of bondage.

The last year has shown how profound is the need, how widespread the desire, for basic change in the United States. The rage of working people and the unemployed, of women, of people of color, has not yet produced the level of organization and unity that can force basic change. But with so much dissatisfaction and pain, the political landscape is likely to take on a very different aspect over the next several years.

Whatever socialists can contribute (and should without stint), socialist ideas and organizations are necessarily in a tentative stage at present. We have to be open to the fact that socialist alternatives will emerge in a variety of ways, from a variety of movements. They will take on life and political form if the demand for fundamental change grips the consciousness of working people. The birth, or rebirth, of socialist inspiration in the United States is inherent in the

search that many Americans are beginning to feel deeply—
that there must be a better way to live...

PART III

NEW TERRAIN

CHAPTER 9

NOT THE SAME OLD WORLD

I am still addicted to the future, reaching for a sense of where this world may be headed. The attraction is not to predictions, nor even to indulging fond hopes, but to possibilities. As the hero of the play, *Jacobowsky and the Colonel*, repeated in every circumstance, "there are always two possibilities." At least!

If possibilities are divided broadly into two categories, the good and the bad, making a case for the former may seem today like fantasy or simply naiveté. Who can ignore the road signs that point to disaster? Even though the primary peril of extinction through nuclear war is diminished by the end of the Cold War, survival of life on earth remains at issue as it never has before in human history. The most striking fact about the Twentieth Century is that humanity acquired the technological capacity to destroy itself completely and to make our planet uninhabitable. There is so far no reason for assurance that society can save itself.

In the immediate aftermath of the Cold War, there is sickening proof that every kind of tragedy and all forms of bestiality remain to defile humanity. Somalia, Iraq, the former Yugoslavia, Haiti, and countless other places of terrible suffering confirm that we are not nearly finished with war and genocide, with racism, rape and starvation. Within the United States, mindless euphoria over the military might displayed in the Gulf War has faded. There was soon less inclination to cheer and more reason to worry about what is happening here: about a declining economy and unemployment, about chronic deterioration of cities and schools, about the portent of events that exploded around the Rodney King verdict, about ultra-Right assaults on fundamental human rights, about incredible levels of violence and misery that ruin so many lives.

If I do not intend to concentrate on the tragic and perilous in human affairs, it is only because that picture is drawn for us so convincingly by every day's news. Is there something else to see, other possibilities? And are they more substantial than the product of wishful thinking?

The question for me is whether the world has changed in fundamental ways during the last half century, and whether the changes carry positive, in addition to their obvious negative, potential for human destiny.

The most remarkable changes are scientific and technological. Revolutions in technology have a profound relevance to humanity's fate, but the ultimate determination rests with society itself. There is nothing intrinsic in any new technology that determines the balance between possible constructive and destructive consequences. However, the enormous technological changes fostered by post-World War II capitalism have altered the ways of the world in economics, culture, and politics. They have changed significantly the way the capitalist system functions. Production is organized increasingly on a multinational basis in a global economy. In the developed capitalist countries, service and communications operations have extended the work force while diminishing its traditional industrial sector.

The compounded results of technological advance, especially in computer science and communications, are creating a small world, with people and nations interconnected and interdependent as never before. Integration, however, does not equal community. If anything, the global reach of prevailing economic structures, and the multimedia dissemination of information and propaganda, make more apparent the unequal circumstances and polarizing antagonisms that separate people within and among nations.

Capitalism is dominant at the end of the Twentieth Century and, contrary to earlier predictions of most Marxists, its demise is not imminent. Yet, a fundamental insight by Marx defines today's world. The social character of the society shaped by modern capitalism is increasingly in conflict with capitalism's essential nature, with the motivation and methods of the "private enterprise" system. Now, as humanity copes with potentially overwhelming challenges, the unprecedented requirements of social responsibility collide forcefully with "normal" capitalist logic and morality.

The conflict between capitalism and "its" society has been present from the beginning of the industrial revolution. It is documented in the early history of bitter struggles for a reasonable working day and for the regulation of child labor. Competition for profits has been a powerful deterrent to consideration by individual capitalists and capitalist governments of the long term social consequences of their conduct. "Hence," wrote Karl Marx, "Capital is reckless of the health or length of life of the labourer, unless under compulsion from society" (*Capital*, Volume I, 296, Kerr Edition, 1906). Such compulsion, propelled by labor struggles and organization, is at the core of every social advance in modern history. The paradox is that the need to respond to "compulsion from society" has served to save capitalism from itself, opening avenues of escape from the consequences of the crises it generates.

Nevertheless, at the end of the Twentieth Century, the tension between society and the pursuit of blind greed stretches far beyond struggles over conditions of labor. It has now become the determinant of humanity's fate.

What can that tension produce in an era when capitalist interests dominate global economic activity even more decisively than during the Cold War? Can it prevent a final calamitous rerun of the political history of the first half of the twentieth century, the time of world wars and the fascist plague? Can it reverse the destruction of the environment? Can it reduce mass hunger and poverty? Can it open the doors to political and economic equity for the excluded and oppressed majority of the world's population?

Most socialists have argued, and some still do, that the only alternative to catastrophe is the end of capitalism. I would argue that time rules out so absolute an alternative. The issues of human survival have matured more rapidly than long term possibilities for a revolutionary termination of capitalism. The alternative that may instead prove possible within the next few decades is the erosion of capitalism's monopoly over political, economic and social power, the rupture of its strangle-hold on society's destiny. That depends on the potential strength of an array of social forces with the will to confront today's life or death problems, and whose vital interests demand significant access to power.

Can an effective world community develop that differs from the "new world order" heralded by Bush, which was predicated on US military super power and the global economic dictatorship of the G7? Only an agnostic response to that question is credible for now.

To put first questions first, though, what can we make of the few countries now experiencing a significant democratic advance where, a few years ago, oppression appeared absolute and interminable? I think South Africa and El Salvador tell us a lot about the struggle for social change in today's world: the awesome difficulties and inconclusive results, but also the ingredients that make it possible to overcome. Both countries are in the throes of historic transition from an horrendous past to a hopeful, but uncertain future. The primary ingredient of progress in both cases is the unflagging, heroic, and costly struggle of an oppressed people against a ferocious reactionary state, whose power was sustained for many years by dominant imperialist allies, especially by the United States. The turning point came with a changed international situation, in which outside support for Apartheid or a military-feudal oligarchy became increasingly untenable and outside pressure for social justice became more assertive. Without both the indigenous struggle and effective support within the international community, significant social change would not be achievable or, at least, not sustainable.

The boundless chaos that erupted with the end of the Cold War may settle into a more comprehensible, though unstable equilibrium. Problems and disputes that in the world's present state remain beyond fundamental solution, nevertheless become approachable out of the sheer necessity to reduce human suffering and stop the descent to social collapse. Some advances are far more important than others, but all are compromises and none escape the disappointments and obstacles imposed by an unjust and dominant capitalist world system. This is evident in the historic, but still unequal, mutual recognition agreement between the Israeli government and the PLO, but it applies also to countries and regions where popular forces have achieved a more favorable balance in power relationships. Even where the compromises reflect a heroic popular victory, they do not bring about a just society and may not directly improve the lot of the poor and exploited.

Without minimizing hard won progress toward democracy, the prospects for basic social and economic advances in any one country will remain bleak without political changes that effectively challenge the power that multinational corporations exert over domestic and global affairs. I won't try to speculate on the processes by which new social and economic forms will intrude on and eventually rupture capitalism's domination of humanity's fate. For some time, the question will be how to open some doors to diversity in arenas where issues of global significance are "managed," how to introduce a degree of representation (of pluralism) that goes beyond the common objectives as well as the antagonisms of the main industrial powers. That is the counterpart of struggles to open the doors to serious democratic participation in country after country where economic and military elites have ruled closed societies.

In time, strivings for social justice and progress within nations have to converge in cooperative efforts to create new conditions and combinations internationally that correct the extreme power imbalance that followed the end of the Cold War.

February 2, 1994:

When I started writing this book in the winter of 1991, I felt that time and circumstance would soon give me authentic clues to the future. I kept the first two sections skeleton trim, because I was anxious to get beyond the past to "new terrain," where my hopes and thoughts wanted to be. I wrote without much interruption what I thought would serve as a personal introduction to my effort to fathom the present and to recognize cross currents propelling social progress.

Since then, and for many months now, I have stalled. I have not been waiting for the outcome of one or many of the great dramas, mostly tragedies, that fill the world's stage. Rather, I have tried to fight off the realization that processes making for a different and significantly better future remain largely hidden, at least from me.

The problem is not the loss of hope or a lack of ideas. It's that the gap between necessity and the visible potential for social change is still so vast. One can verify the need for fundamental change in economic and political institutions, worldwide and in the USA, and one can identify a potentially transforming power centered in the mass of humanity that is desperate for change. But the movement of events that might eventually bridge the enormous power imbalance between "haves" and "have-nots" cannot be foretold, nor can the forms of social change that such historic movement would produce.

So, I will put aside efforts to complete this manuscript. At least for the present, it will remain unfinished. I will write articles, as I have been doing, but without the notion that I can satisfy the compulsion that keeps me "looking for the future." There are so many things to write about, mulling over the obstacles to social change in the United States, supporting struggles for justice here and elsewhere. I also want to write more about social and scientific aspects of the "genetic revolution," as I expected to do in the last chapter of this book.

On this Ground Hog Day, I think I must accept that Winter is far from over. Manifestations of Spring are still below the surface.

March 30, 1994:

Spring is here, by the calendar, not yet the political season. Maybe I can carry this manuscript through to a less abrupt finale after all, if I resist looking around each corner for the "light at the end of the tunnel."

During the interlude after I abruptly curtailed my little book, friends read the unfinished product and encouraged me to take it further. What I have already written won't be changed, at least not substantially. Even the italicized notes that mark the pause remain, so that I can share some of my hesitation. I am switching gears, however, in the concluding portion. Having accepted my inability to project the future, I will just express some thoughts on a few problems "in the here and now."

This will remain a short book. I resist suggestions to turn it into a more elaborate personal memoir. I also don't want to write more extensively about the Communist experience and legacy. I prefer to limit myself to expressing my main thoughts and reactions—if readers want to fill in the gaps or ask many questions I leave hanging, so much the better. If I convey my own feelings, and stimulate the memories and thinking of others, I don't mind leaving the agenda incomplete.

Perhaps a "proper" ending to this chapter on our changed world is an article in which I tried to take a post-Cold War look at issues of intervention and international efforts to stop murderous wars:

ON INTERVENTION

Published in CrossRoads, *No. 33, July/August 1993*

Since the end of the Cold War, debates on intervention (who should intervene, why, where and when) have become murkier than ever. Last year the focus was Somalia, the Persian Gulf before that, and now the argument rages over Bosnia with unmatched bitterness and frustration.

For forty years after the end of the Second World War, the many encounters involving foreign interventions were dominated by two considerations: the Cold War strategies of the competing superpowers, and the potential that regional conflicts might bring on nuclear war. That is not to diminish the underlying causes of conflict that devastated so many countries, particularly the oppression and suffering that ignited popular struggles against colonial rule, racist regimes and military oligarchies. Presidents of the United States, Republican and Democrat, justified the risks of intervention— from the declaration of the Truman Doctrine in Europe, the wars in Korea and Vietnam, to the pursuit of the Contra War in Central America—as necessary to the strategy of countering the Soviet peril. At critical points along the way, however, US and Soviet leaders pulled back from ultimate acts of confrontation that could initiate nuclear war.

For progressives devoted to peace, there was a clear rationale for opposing imperialistic military interventions that used the Cold War to bolster oppressive regimes, and that chanced escalation to a third world war. Now no common denominator is apparent. Everything seems much more complex and ambiguous. Erstwhile opponents of US military intervention during the 1980s, in Central America and elsewhere, now hurl brickbats at each other over what to do about Bosnia.

The problems that have exploded to the surface in the post-Cold War world are horrendous. Circumstances abound that demand the forceful attention and action of an enlightened world community—but where and how is that to be found?

It certainly will not evolve from the concept of a "new world order" predicated on the United States, as the sole remaining military superpower, serving as global police chief. No one can believe that the application of US force will subdue the torrents of ethnic and religious hatreds fomented in Europe, Africa, and Asia, any more than such action can answer the massive problems of starvation, the rampant flow of murderous armaments, the floods of refugees, or ubiquitous assaults on the environment.

Nevertheless, the end of the Cold War does increase the possibility that the United States can be involved in more constructive ways on issues of global concern. The extent to which that happens will depend on the relative weight of deeply contradictory interests that influence US foreign policy. The United States is inescapably connected to the universal concerns about humanity's fate that dominate the horizon of the twenty first century. We have both reason and potential to join in collective actions to promote nego-tiated and democratic solutions to conflicts, to aid victims of famine, war or genocide, to combat disease and curb pollu-tion. However, the economic and political interests of US capital also remain inseparably connected to a dominant international system that deepens chasms of inequality, misery and injustice, and that renders impotent efforts to achieve genuine world community. Appeals to global conscience and responsibility ring hollow when the G7 industrial nations hold the monopoly on real power, and whenever unilateral US military initiative and command are imposed on the United Nations.

From these considerations, it makes no sense automatically to oppose US involvement in any foreign crisis or dispute as inherently evil. Equally, it would be unconscionable for progressives to support unilateral military intervention by the United States anywhere, even if the UN can be pressured into giving its reluctant sanction. Issues that ought to be considered in every case are: What kind of help is needed from the international community, including from the United States? What role can the US play that strengthens, rather than weakens, collective action and the United Nations? Will the measures undertaken (and the burdens) put priority on the interests of the people, at home and abroad, rather than on advancement of multinational corporate interests?

Intervention through a wide range of collective measures is a necessary response to more than a few crisis situations, but outright acts of war aimed at imposing military "solutions" from the outside ought to be avoided as a plague. Nowhere do military invasions and bombings solve conflicts fueled by nationalist and religious antagonisms. They only increase the toll in lives and in hopes for a better life. Above all, they continue to legitimate war in a world which has now acquired the capacity to self-destruct. Massive US "search and destroy" missions against Khaddafy in Tripoli, Saddam in Baghdad, and Aidid in Mogadishu failed spectacularly to eliminate their human "surgical" targets, brought havoc rather than solutions, and inspired hatred among horrified populations. It is past time to relegate military actions to the status of last resort, when aggression or extreme provocation makes such responses unavoidable, limited in scope to the needs of the situation, and always taking into account the collective interest and will of the United Nations.

The purpose of this article is not to examine the causes of disaster in the Balkans, the claims of any side, or historic and recent contributions of great powers to the bloody impasse. Today there are powerful reasons for collective intervention to end the nightmare in Bosnia, to employ the pressure of the international community to stop the murderous artillery assaults, the mass executions and rapes that have engulfed dismembered Yugoslavia. There is every need and justification for heavy sanctions, UN protection for humanitarian operations to feed beleaguered populations and save refugees, the promise of punishment for war crimes, and the most persistent efforts for an effective cease fire and serious negotiations, including possible agreement on a temporary presence for UN peace-keeping forces.

Anthony Lewis and Christopher Hitchens are liberals who demand a different course. They say Europe has defaulted shamefully and the US must intervene, taking strong military action in support of Bosnia's Muslims against the Serbs. Both berate Clinton for indecisiveness in refusing to go it alone, and Hitchens calls *The Nation,* to which he contributes a regular column, "contemptible" for opposing his position.

Lewis and Hitchens argue that what's happening in Bosnia is analogous to the Nazi Holocaust, and thus they justify subordinating, if not discarding, all other considerations. As horrible as are the atrocities by warring factions in the former Yugoslavia (and as terrifying as is genocidal warfare in areas of Africa and Asia) it is reckless folly to disregard whether unilateral US military intervention will worsen rather than improve matters. Moreover, the ready analogies often made to the era of Hitler's Third Reich (applied by Bush to Saddam in Iraq, and even to Noriega in Panama) can be a dangerous misreading of history.

What justified, in fact ultimately required, the world alliance for war against Hitler, was that the Fascist Axis of Germany, Japan, and Italy was pursuing a war to conquer the world. That hardly is what we see today when we look at the Balkans or Sudan or Cambodia. Could collective measures short of war have stopped Hitler soon after he took power, and thus aborted or prevented the Holocaust? Britain, France, and The United States never agreed to a collective security policy in concert with the USSR until after World War II was underway. Perhaps if they supported, rather than boycotted, the legitimate governments of Spain and Ethiopia, if they applied strong sanctions against Germany before Hitler's Third Reich was firmly consolidated, his regime could have been thrown into crisis and opposition forces might have been able to mount a challenge. In any case, the argument for collective security even at that time was not to rush to apply war measures, but the hope that a united world community could stop fascism and prevent world war.

We return to the fact that there is nothing more necessary today than the emergence of an enlightened, strong, peaceful and democratic world community. We are a long way from it. All the more reason to think about how to get there, and to strive for it, even desperately, but with patience and conviction. The end of the Cold War exemplified the possibility, but what has happened since threatens to keep it out of reach. Probably the greatest strategic set-back was the failure of historic efforts to transform the USSR into a democratic socialist world power. Such a development could have favored the aspirations of the "have-not" nations and peoples of the world for greater equity and diversity in the international arena. Instead, the collapse of the Soviet Union produced fragmentation and a spreading inferno of ethnic and nationalist hatreds, leaving international capitalist interests supreme.

Hope for the future depends more than ever on popular struggles to change the world, not least of all the USA. That vision anticipates breaking down the monopoly of selfish corporate interests over economic and political power, so that humanity can come together to attend to its needs. How that will happen, we cannot yet tell, but necessity remains the mother of invention.

Along the way, even in the uncertain world of today, international solidarity and collective action through the United Nations can have a significant impact. Such efforts, which include bringing about some changes in long-standing US policies, have facilitated vital, if partial, democratic advances gained by powerful movements in El Salvador, South Africa, and Guatemala. Evident also is the capacity, given sufficient will and pressure, to restore Haiti's democratically elected government. In the deeply troubling aftermath of the Cold War, a most urgent challenge is to promote ceaseless, wide-ranging, international unity to stop violent crusades for ethnic and religious supremacy. But another stab at a "quick fix" by way of US military superpower can only extend the tragedy.

CHAPTER 10

CHANGING POLITICS IN THE USA

In this second Clinton year, a lot is being learned about
the battle for social change—how badly it is needed and how
hard it is to pull free of the quicksand that sucks at every
forward movement.

In the early months of the new administration, many of
my friends argued over what Bill Clinton is about. Most, even
those who hoped for the best, were soon jolted into disappointment and anger. The list is long of retreats on principle,
of overtures to conservatism and put-downs against labor and
civil rights constituencies. To give but four examples: the
abrupt dismissal of Lani Guinier and her views on minority
representation; overriding of labor's concerns about NAFTA
(on no other issue has he exerted such vigorous and uncom-
promising effort); his prolonged insistence on forcibly turning
over Haitian refugees to a murderous, outlaw regime; his per-
petuation of cruel and exceptional policies aimed at starving
out Cuban independence.

Yet that damning litany is not the full measure of the man,
of his policies or, more important, of the problems preventing
significant social progress. I don't think the cardinal question

is about Clinton and his intentions. It is about the political process, whether it can be shifted so that we can cope with our most urgent economic and social problems. Whatever Clinton's failings, the bigger message is the resistance to social justice and progress that is embedded in our political system, nurtured by most of the media and by years of aggressive conservative influence on public attitudes. On those issues where Clinton has tried to act on campaign promises, most notably his and Hillary's push for universal health coverage, the counter attack mobilized by big money interests has been ferocious. The general assault on the Clintons *per se* is without limits in decency or relevance to serious issues.

Even though the country voted down the Reagan-Bush regime in favor of change, the power balance and prevailing political culture remain stacked against a positive break with the status quo. There is a broad political convergence from the Right, regardless of distinctions between groups, that emerges whenever any proposition for social and/or economic justice threatens. Clinton's colleagues in the Democratic Leadership Council (Nunn and Boren, to name two) are usually in step with the Republican Party of Dole and Gingrich, the Perot phalanx, and the "Christian" armies of Robertson and Falwell in ganging up against jobs programs, gay rights, immigrants, the appointment of civil rights advocates, abortion rights for poor women, environmental protection measures, and the establishment of universal health care. Behind this informal consortium is enormous financial power in advertising and the media—the blitz against health reform by the insurance and pharmaceutical industries is only the most obvious example.

There is no comparable convergence in favor of a serious program to deal with the deteriorating economic and social plight of most Americans. There certainly are strong social movements on many particular problems, but the power of coming together to move the country forward is lacking. Over the last two or three decades, unifying initiatives around political programs for social change have usually emerged in presidential election periods, sometimes showing great potential strength and spirit, but with little of consequence surviving beyond the primary campaigns.

There are reasons aplenty for the lack of effective linkage between social movements and for the inability to create an ongoing political force for progressive change: the political and electoral system is structured to discourage independent expression and representation for populist movements; corporate wealth monopolizes the media and distorts the democratic process at every level; the labor movement has been weakened by economic restructuring and years of retreat under reactionary attack; racism divides and alienates natural allies as problems connected to economic and social inequality seem intractable; the political culture carried over from the 1980s undermines expectations that government can or should do something constructive about people's needs.

Can political prospects be changed for the better before they revert again to worse, as, for example, in the return of another Reagan-Bush (Gingrich-Dole?) type presidency?

There is no single formula that unlocks the solution to independent political action and progressive unity. Granted, only a third populist force can counter and overcome the frustrations inherent in the closed two-party system. Yet little is accomplished by arguments that seek the "correct" answer in setting up a "third party" versus reliance on forces for change within the Democratic Party. Neither of these formulas define the major movements that have pressed the country forward in my lifetime, the response to the Great Depression and to fascism in the Thirties, and the uprising against Jim Crow in the Fifties and Sixties. These unity movements became powerful enough to force change in traditional politics and power structures, even though they didn't fashion permanent, institutional answers to two-party control. Perhaps movements of the future will change US politics more significantly, but that would have to be the product of broad, new experience and strength in unity rather than doctrinaire confrontations between "tendencies" on the Left.

Some guidelines occur to me. (One of the risks of aging is that one may take on the manner of a sage, not always consciously, when the accumulated experience of a lifetime suggests modesty and uncertainty.)

Even though we may not now be able to predict the process of birth or the form of new unifying progressive formations, we can recognize something of the spirit and outlook required for their cultivation. For one thing, there is something to be learned from the strength of the Right in our politics and culture. Its constituencies vary widely in style, focus, and doctrinal loyalties, but they are bound by a *common purpose*—to prevent any progressive turn in the country's direction. For progressives, a spirit of *common purpose*—with the opposite objective—is more important than inevitable differences on issues, priorities, and political methods.

Criticism and public debate are unavoidable, and absolutely necessary. But the slings and arrows of accusation and self-righteousness blind us to the many-sided efforts, the multiplicity of approaches, needed to win the country to a change of course. Groups committed to social change may choose one way of politics over another, and seek to gain support, but different and seemingly contradictory approaches can actually share in moving the process forward. Every effective popular movement has varied components, some favoring the most inclusive activities and coalition building, and others pursuing independent organization and militant actions. Sometimes these currents are at variance, sometimes they overlap. I can think of many examples of this interaction, and no exceptions, among the movements that have moved multitudes and changed public perceptions on one or another set of issues: the crusade against Jim Crow, the women's movement, the movement for gay rights, and more. Pushing and pulling, sometimes confronting, sometimes inspiring, these movements—as the sum of their parts—have changed the thinking of millions. Despite adverse conditions, they have opened up the social and political culture of the nation to new values and expectations.

Still, far more is needed to change the overall reality of local and national politics.

While a majority of Americans feel that something is very wrong (some would say fundamentally wrong), anger and frustration are diffused and misdirected by "opinion makers" (endless talk shows, TV pundits and evangelists, political commercials). The outlook for change, nevertheless, derives from the reality that present policies cannot cope with society's crisis problems, cannot even preserve the *status quo*. The history of previous uphill battles shows that when things are badly enough out of whack, people who hurt find their voices and create new alternatives despite the demagogues.

Today's social movements, some well-organized and others exploring ways to come together, are likely to spawn new means of political organization locally and nationally. My guess is that the most successful initiatives will be committed both to political independence and to the formation of coalitions unrestricted by party labels. Independence means the right to criticize candidates and elected officials and to advance better programs and ideas. Silence in the name of political loyalty is a formula for impotence. Neither is it sensible to turn a disagreement or criticism into a general condemnation of progressive or liberal politicians. One can recognize that expediency is to some extent a code for everyone in politics, and that politics requires compromise, without impugning the courage or integrity of anyone who steps into the political arena.

Since the mold of the two party system so confines democratic electoral expression, changing the way the game is played will demand political creativity as well as a major upheaval by voters and non-voters alike. Perhaps grass-roots political action organizations or coalitions will come about, somewhat akin in form to Perot's movement or to progressive formations of earlier eras that arose in several states and municipalities. Such independent political creations would not be bound by any party organization or hierarchy, yet would participate in every possible way in shaping legislative programs and conventions, choosing candidates, affecting electoral campaigns, and monitoring performance of government. They would sponsor local efforts to expand political representation, especially for the most oppressed and excluded populations. The kind of proposals explored by Lani Guinier for varied forms of proportional representation could begin to crack the prevailing political mold.

How far any serious political innovation might proceed depends on how powerful are the upheavals that give it energy. One can't predict earthquakes with any accuracy, in society any more than in nature. Yet the fault lines are recognizable in intolerable social and economic conditions that cripple the lives and hopes of millions of children and youth, most of all among people of color, and that deprive more and more workers of security and opportunity. Political reality is not defined by abstract principles proclaiming what is or is not possible, but can instead be shaped by the strength and will of popular movements. A movement that gains powerful support will write the democratic agenda of which it is capable, without accepting limits in advance: neither the proposition that "the Democratic Party can never be won to popular control" nor that "the system will never permit a successful new party." In appropriate circumstances, the politically impossible can happen. (There are pertinent civics lessons this year—worlds apart from our social context—in South Africa, where "people power" and remarkable political flexibility are joined; in Brazil, where the grass-roots Workers' Party has achieved great political strength; in Mexico, where the Zapatistas have roused a nation despite the ruling party's entrenched power monopoly.)

In these unsettled and unsettling circumstances, there are groups and individuals who hope to renew socialist traditions that are part of US labor history. I believe there is need for socialist ideals and ideas, for the proven dedication of socialist activists to battles for justice, for critical dissection of capitalism's nature and direction, for promoting the principle of worldwide labor solidarity against racism and exploitation, and for innovative thinking about socialist solutions to the crisis problems of our times. I don't think those contributions can be forthcoming from any sect with its own restrictive claim to socialist "truth." Several socialist organizations and publications are seeking new non-sectarian ground; among them, the Democratic Socialists of America has attracted and retained the most representative national sponsorship.

A broad association of democratic socialists would have something attractive and worthwhile to offer. It could be effective and influential, even though relatively small at present, if it cultivated an ecumenical spirit. It would respect the continuity of socialist values represented variously in our history by Eugene Debs, W.E.B. Du Bois, Mother Jones, Michael Harrington, William Foster, Norman Thomas, C.L.R. James, Gurley

Flynn, Albert Einstein, Martin L. King Jr., Caesar Chavez, Malcolm X, Lucy Parsons, Paul Robeson, and Upton Sinclair. It would have to be more than intellectual, actively involved with current issues and vital local movements. And it would also have to be modest, never conceiving of itself as the primary vehicle for shaking up and changing politics in the USA.

CHAPTER 11

GENES AND DESTINY

One might think that when I became a molecular biologist I was in the right place at the right time to satisfy my addiction to the future. James Watson, who with Francis Crick, won the Nobel Prize for solving the riddle of DNA structure, has said: "We used to think our fate was in our stars. Now we know, in large measure, our fate is in our genes." (Quoted in *Time*, "The Gene Hunt," by Leon Jaroff, March 20, 1989.)

But three hundred and ninety years earlier, Shakespeare, speaking through Cassius in *Julius Caesar*, already knew that our fate was not in our stars:

> "Men at some time are masters of their fates:
> The fault, dear Brutus, is not in our stars,
> But in ourselves, that we are underlings."

Ruling out the stars, then, do genes determine our destiny? Or may people be "masters of their fates?" How that conundrum is interpreted will affect, for better or worse, the meaning of the "genetic revolution" for society.

The *Time* article quoting Watson is a grand representation of the Human Genome Project, "a $3 billion project to map the chromosomes and decipher the complete instructions for making a human being." It is described as: "a monumental effort that could rival in scope both the Manhattan Project, which created the A-bomb, and the Apollo moon-landing program—and may exceed them in importance." A dramatic center-spread diagram of an infant outlined in helical coils of DNA asks: "What will this baby be? Football star? Scholar? Rock guitarist?..."

Why does this picture upset me? Why does commercialized hype over "genetic engineering" and "biotechnology" bother some biologists who, like me, consider the breakthrough in molecular genetics to be one of the most significant intellectual and scientific achievements of our age?

First, because it cloaks the reality that most of humanity is consigned to conditions that waste body and mind, that deny genetic potential. Second, because it implies a technological "fix" for most problems of health and even, some suggest, of behavior.

The Twentieth Century has experienced more than a few revolutions in technology. They change our lives and enlarge human potential enormously, for better and for worse. In turn, society puts its stamp on technological revolutions, their uses and their consequences. The nature of the social order—its priorities, values, strengths, and weaknesses—is the primary determinant of how people are affected by breakthroughs in science and technology. The advent of the nuclear age changed, but didn't "fix" society's problems. The wonders of the computer revolution keep changing how everything is done, but actually accentuate the disparity of educational opportunity between rich and poor. "Genetic engineering" opens vistas of innovation in medicine, agriculture, and numerous other fields, but its blessings, too, are not unmixed. Nor is it the cure-all for disease, either medically or in regard to underlying social ills.

To appreciate the "genetic revolution" properly, it seems to me essential to reject genetic *determinism*, for reasons of both science and society. The quotes I use around "genetic revolution" are there because the historic discoveries concerning DNA and genes are inseparable from remarkable advances in the whole area of molecular and cell biology—our knowledge of antibodies, enzymes, and hormones, of how cells are constructed, of some cellular processes and interactions, of the complex workings of the immune system, and more. The information encoded in genes is fundamental to life and development, yet there are many variables affecting how, when, and what information is expressed or modified. Some variables are intrinsic to the DNA, some arise within the biological environment from the inception of an organism's development, and the external environment influences the organism profoundly throughout its lifetime. In turn, such understanding is not a rejection of the role of heredity in shaping all aspects of an individual.

The ability to read DNA sequences, to locate genes on chromosomes, to splice and synthesize genes in the laboratory, to introduce genes into cells and cause them to produce a particular enzyme or other protein—these developments have indeed revolutionized biological research and opened the way to new insights into all life processes, into cancer and numerous diseases. The more that is learned, the more likely is the emergence of new approaches in areas of medicine. Whatever medical miracles may appear, and some will, the complexities of life and the environment will not surrender to a one-front genetic war. Modern society, despite one contemporary prophet, has not reached "the end of history," the pinnacle of social development; nor has the millennium come, by virtue of the "genetic revolution," for medicine and the biological sciences.

To hear some publicists for biotechnology (including scientists) tell it, health problems are primarily genetic and the new tools will provide the solution. They herald a "paradigm shift" in how health and disease are understood and dealt with. *Time* (ibid.) quotes a scientist in the Human Genome Office of the National Institutes of Health: "Eventually people might have access to a computer readout of their own genome, with an interpretation of their genetic strengths and weakness. At the very least this would enable them to adopt an appropriate life-style, choosing the proper diet, environment and—if necessary—drugs to minimize the effects of genetic disorders."

The scientifically misleading aspects of that assessment are too numerous and complex for serious treatment here. A few things to consider are: 1) The Genome Project, when completed years from now, will at best give us a prototype genome, whereas genomes vary with each individual. 2) As huge as is the task of determining the *make-up* of some 100,000 prototype human genes, discovering the *role* of each and every one is presently beyond even imagination. 3) In the few cases where a gene can be identified with the product it encodes, and where a particular form(s) of the gene is linked to a given disease, implications for therapy usually remain obscure.

These major reservations do not belie the possible value of genetic information about individuals, families, population groups, and the species. Such information can be developed more readily and reliably as new biochemical techniques are combined with the range of available methods in genetic research.

The most staggering fallacy, however, is the paradigm that approaches the health problem as essentially a matter of genetics. One need only a glance at the actual status of health in the United States, not to speak of the health of the "disadvantaged" vast majority of the world's population. The overwhelming causes of sickness, disease, suffering, and untimely death lie not in the individual genome, but in the human condition. Of course, being born into poverty, in a poor country or in a ghetto, and without access to decent health care, can be correlated statistically to categories of race and ethnicity. But that is a matter of society, of deeply imbedded inequalities unmitigated by progress in genetics.

Sociologist Troy Duster, in his book *Eugenics by the Back Door* (Routledge, 1990), makes the point by way of an example: "The lung cancer rate among blacks has soared in five decades, and since human gene pools cannot change so rapidly, no one can argue that this is a function of a changing genetic susceptibility. Rather, the 39,000 blacks who died in 1986 from smoking-related diseases did so in large measure because the black smoking rate is higher than the white smoking rate, and in part because blacks are more likely to be employed in occupations and industries with high levels of environmental pollutants, and four times more likely to live in poverty—a combination of factors that just happen to 'coincide' with the last half-century of shifting race-related cancer rates."

Serious reform of the health system, assuring universal and equal access, is one necessary element of social change if the advances in biology and medicine are to mean what they should for society. Unfortunately, some molecular biologists, physicians, psychologists, and sociologists are less concerned with social reform than with promoting genetics as the key to social problems, such as crime, alcoholism, homelessness, drug addiction, violence, and lack of education. The ideology that groups of humans could be categorized according to superior or inferior genetic endowment should have disappeared with Hitler. Yet euphoric fantasies triggered by the rise of molecular genetics seem to offer, through a mix of bad "science" and social irresponsibility, a new opening for pseudo-eugenic theories.

Most molecular biologists would reject as simple-minded the effort to extrapolate "evidence" for genetic determinism from their research. However, their disengagement with the public allows (and some even contribute to) misconceptions fed by propaganda from biotechnology and pharmaceutical sources that eagerly exploit a major new market. *Science*, our most important general research journal for scientists, has been notorious in its editorial speculations on genetic answers to social problems, presented amid a forest of ads from manufacturers of biotechnology equipment.

Having been on both sides of the divide between scientist and layman, I have thought a lot about science and social responsibility. Should the public expect scientists to do the right thing, to be candid, patiently informative, concerned about the impact of their work on people's lives and on social policy?

My experience over several decades gives me respect for the personal integrity and decency of most of my colleagues in immunology and molecular biology. Moreover, quite a number of biological scientists were among the most outspoken academic opponents of the Vietnam War; many gave support to affirmative action for women and people of color, and to student efforts to make the university more democratic. There is no doubt, though, that the prevailing culture has changed since molecular biology became a great new frontier for business investment and speculation. The love for research remains, but the preoccupations are largely of a different sort. Virtually all significant researchers have formed vital connections with biotechnology enterprises. Predictably, in their university laboratories, there is more secrecy, a more restrictive environment for students, and more focus on projects that may generate patents and entrepreneurial investment.

It would be somewhat unfair to admonish individual researchers for what was probably an inevitable economic and social outcome. What should be recognized, however, is that conflicts of interest have become the norm at the very time when the public needs to understand and act on social, ethical, and health issues brought forward by advances in genetic techniques. We are also at a juncture where reawakening of the earlier social responsibility could contribute mightily to countering the resistance of drug and insurance conglomerates to serious health reform.

One problem connects most clearly the issues of reforming the health system and of social policy toward the "genetic revolution." That is the mushrooming phenomenon of genetic testing. Marketing reagents and equipment for this purpose is one of the most lucrative fields in biotechnology. I won't discuss here the incentive for unnecessary tests, or ethical issues concerning the validity of some tests or their effect on the individual tested. Rather, I want to pursue the question of employer and insurance company interest in widespread genetic testing.

The selling rationale for subjecting workers to arrays of genetic, drug, HIV, and other tests is that they may tell the employer the "risk" that a given employee could get sick or break down on the job. That, in turn, is supposed to allow the employer to figure in the potential effects on his insurance costs of his hiring and phase out (firing) decisions. Leaving aside that many such tests are flagrantly misleading rather than predictive, the testing game compounds the incredible injustice of a health system that already funnels every aspect of an individual's health problems and needs through the computers of the insurance industry. It looks like the "computer readouts" of genetic information anticipated so eagerly in some Human Genome Project promotions will belong not to the individual, but to those who hold veto power over the individual's well-being—unless health reform eventually guarantees universal access and care in a system that excludes the insurance industry and its "risk" (discrimination) calculations.

Molecular genetics and cell biology will continue to open new doors to understanding and, in some respects, dealing with cancer, AIDS, and diseases that plague humans. But the key measure of progress in human health—and the health of society—will not be the speed with which we fill in the maps of the Human Genome Project. Rather, it will be how far society moves toward a revolution in our health system, guaranteeing decent health care as a universal human right.

June 7, 1994:

This is as far as my little book goes. Pages back, if not from the beginning, it was obvious that I couldn't yet find the future that socialist theorists, idealists, and activists dreamed of and fought for. If I needed a reminder, however, of the importance of their ideas, actions, and inspiration for the past, present, and future, it came while I was writing these last chapters. It came in South Africa, an essential part of one of the most glorious episodes of human liberation. Destiny remains to be determined, the post-capitalist future to be defined through the sum of human experience in quest of a just society.

I think that destiny will be fashioned not by James Watson's formula, "Our fate is in our genes," but by that of Karl Marx and Frederick Douglass, in the latter's words: "If there is no struggle, there is no progress."

CHAPTER 12

POSTSCRIPT

The several months that passed, while I was arranging publication of *Looking for the Future,* have brought the Congressional elections of 1994. The political pendulum had barely begun its swing away from Reaganism when it was forced roughly back to the Right.

No nationwide election campaign in my memory has been ruled more blatantly by fortunes, personal and corporate. Again, a majority of the small voting portion (39%) of the electorate—more white and male and, on average, more "middle class" than the general population—has been egged on to blame our problems on scapegoats. Never have as many politicians directed as much hatred against ordinary people: mothers on welfare; immigrants and their children; the poor and the homeless; millions of young people of color, left without hope and targeted for punishment.

A few weeks before the elections, Murray and Herrnstein's highly-publicized book, *The Bell Curve,* offered the ideological accompaniment to the mean, race-baiting, scapegoating politics of '94. Our society is endangered, they declared, because "demographic trends are exerting downward pressure on the distribution of cognitive ability in the United States." The poor and, especially, African-Americans, reported an enthusiastic reviewer (*The New York Times Book Review*, October 16, 1994), have "an ineradicable cognitive disability created by genetic bad luck... Worst of all, say the authors, the lowest intellectual levels of the population are strongly outbreeding the brightest... America is losing the cognitive base essential to coping with national problems."

Thus the Gingrich plan to eliminate social programs in favor of prisons and orphanages is not a fiscal matter, but a plan to save America from inferior stock. If that sounds like Nazi eugenics theory, it is. Jensen and Schockley advanced such ideas twenty years ago and fell into disrepute. Now *The Bell Curve* tries again in a climate where memories of eugenic horrors and crimes of racism may be dimming.

So, are we going back, after all, to an earlier era? To the pre-New Deal denial of all social responsibility? To government-fostered racial hatred and persecution of immigrants?

There is no gainsaying the intent of the militant new Congressional leadership and its disciplined ultra-Right constituency. The Democratic Leadership Council will not stand in their way; nor will they be turned back by a weakened and timid President.

What can frustrate them is a ground swell of anger—anger aimed not at scapegoats, but at attempts to twist public outrage into a mandate for attack on the majority of the population. For the moment, there are many Americans who hope they will be better off if the government refuses assistance to the poor, cracks down on immigrants, and jails or executes more criminals. People's sense of self-interest is a strong motivator of political choice, but as recent electoral turnabouts show, perceptions of self-interest can change rapidly if the choice brings misfortune.

Many people see themselves threatened by the social and economic consequences of the Gingrich "Contract." How many more, as their circumstances worsen, will come to see themselves as victims rather than beneficiaries?

Already, there is a growing feeling of shock among millions at the virulence of the arrogant Right. Because most women, most people of color—most people in general—fear or dislike much of their social agenda, the Falwells and Robertsons resort to so-called "stealth" electoral tactics, disguising the affiliations and positions of many of their candidates.

Will enough victims, immediate and potential, fight back? Will they organize to resist, to create an effective political voice, to stop week-kneed politicians from mumbling, "Me, too"? The strong reaction of Latino high school students in California to the anti-immigrant Proposition 187 may be the edge of a wave. It wouldn't be the first time that a new generation upset the arranged political landscape.

And what of our search for the future?

It's too bad that politics confronts us repeatedly with once-won battles to renew. Too bad that history, which records unimaginable changes in the course of a lifetime, moves so slowly toward a vision of social justice. But in every generation, that vision brings hope. It is the source of human brotherhood and sisterhood.